# THE *Heart* OF THE TABLE

Unlocking the treasures to family and community through Sicilian food

**CARMELA AMATO D'AMORE**

The Heart of the Table was first published in 2018

E | info@carmelascucinaclass.com.au
W | www.carmelascucinaclass.com.au
M | 0412 086 111

© Carmela Amato D'Amore 2018

Ordering information

For bulk orders, please contact Carmela via www.carmelascucinaclass.com.au

This book is also available for purchase at Carmela's family restaurant: Sorrento Trattoria, 20 Ocean Beach Road, Sorrento, VIC Australia

 A catalogue record for this book is available from the National Library of Australia.

ISBN: 978-0-9942329-0-8

---

All rights reserved. Except as permitted under The Australian Copyright Act 1968 (for example, a fair dealing for the purposes of study, research, criticism or review), no part of this book may be reproduced, stored in a retrieval system, communicated or transmitted in any form or by any means without prior written permission. All inquiries should be made to the publisher.

Edited by Kate Lloyd
Internal and cover design by Simone Geary
Photography by Beth Jennings
Printed in Australia by Whirlwind Print

10 9 8 7 6 5 4 3 2 1

*This book is dedicated to the families who immigrated from Sicily and left their country to build a new world for their children and their children's children.*

*The heart of the table
begins with you and me;
extending our table
into our community.*

– Carmela D'Amore

# CONTENTS

**ABOUT THE AUTHOR** ............................................................................................................ 6

**FOREWORD BY CATERINA BORSATO** ................................................................................ 7

**INTRODUCTION** ..................................................................................................................... 8

**PART ONE: UNLOCKING THE TREASURE** ......................................................................... 10

    CHAPTER 1 – THE WAY ....................................................................................................... 11

    CHAPTER 2 – THE HEART OF YOUR SEAT ...................................................................... 14

    CHAPTER 3 – THE SPIRIT OF FAMILY ............................................................................... 19

    CHAPTER 4 – EVERY TABLE TELLS A STORY .................................................................. 22

    CHAPTER 5 – A MERE MOTHER; AN IMMIGRANT'S DAUGHTER ............................... 24

    CHAPTER 6 – IS THE TABLE A FADING TRADITION? .................................................... 26

**PART TWO: THE INGREDIENTS OF THE TABLE** ............................................................... 28

    CHAPTER 7 – THE LEGS OF THE TABLE ......................................................................... 30

    CHAPTER 8 – THE HEART OF THE FAMILY .................................................................... 34

    CHAPTER 9 – THE WOMEN OF SICILY ............................................................................ 36

    CHAPTER 10 – WHY I LOVE SICILIAN FOOD ................................................................. 52

**PART THREE: THE MUSIC OF THE TABLE** ......................................................................... 56

    CHAPTER 11 – LET THE MUSIC PLAY ACROSS YOUR TABLE ..................................... 57

    CHAPTER 12 – THE PERFECT RECIPE .............................................................................. 58

    CHAPTER 13 – RECIPES FROM THE HEART ................................................................... 61

    CHAPTER 14 – TRANSFORM YOUR TABLE INTO MUSIC ............................................. 64

    CHAPTER 15 – FAMILY AND HERITAGE .......................................................................... 65

**PART FOUR: THE WEALTH OF THE TABLE** ....................................................................... 68

    CHAPTER 16 – A MEDITATION .......................................................................................... 69

    CHAPTER 17 – SHARING A MEAL ..................................................................................... 70

    CHAPTER 18 – THE HEART OF A WARRIOR .................................................................. 72

    CHAPTER 19 – COURAGE .................................................................................................. 74

    CHAPTER 20 – A JOURNEY THROUGH THE MARKET .................................................. 76

    CHAPTER 21 – I LOVE YOU ................................................................................................ 80

    CHAPTER 22 – WELCOME HOME ..................................................................................... 82

## ABOUT THE AUTHOR

Carmela Amato D'Amore is the daughter and granddaughter of Sicilian immigrants who moved to Australia after World War II. She is the wife of Marco, a mother of four, nonna to three and, amongst that, she is also an international Sicilian chef, president of the lady chefs of the F.I.C delegation of Australia, ambassador of Sicilian food, an author, restaurateur, speaker and storyteller.

Bringing over 40 years of experience to the hospitality industry, Carmela contributes to the community through food and teaching. Her journey has always involved learning and teaching others about food, culture and family. Carmela's first book, *Carmela's Cucina Povera: A journey of self-discovery and healing through Sicilian cooking*, offers over 70 family recipes.

Carmela hosts annual culinary cultural tours of Sicily, continuing the strong connection with her motherland by networking with people and building relationships between the two countries.

In her down time, Carmela can be found reading books or in her garden where she explores her creativity and enjoys spending time with her grandchildren. Carmela currently lives in Victoria, Australia on the Mornington Peninsula and is the executive chef of her family's restaurant, Sorrento Trattoria.

---

### PRAISE FOR *CARMELA'S CUCINA POVERA*

*"Reading Carmela's book echoed my own journey of healing through cooking, especially from the perspective of being from an Italian family in 1960-70s Australia when we desperately wanted to fit in. Her recipes are reminiscent of my mother's cooking and give me feelings of nostalgic comfort."*

— **Teresa Fino,** vibrational alchemist, spiritual mentor, author and speaker

*"Reading Carmela's cherished recipes and her life experiences comforted me to know I wasn't alone. The passion of cooking ignited my life with love, fulfilment and cherished memories with family and friends. Life is full of challenges. But by taking your time and finding the strength to be focused, you can accomplish anything in life. Happiness is food, family and friends."*

— **Sarina Ripepi,** owner of Amoretti Dolce Sweets by Sarina

# FOREWORD BY CATERINA BORSATO

As the daughter of Italian migrants who has lived an Italian life in this very lucky country, I certainly resonate with so much of Carmela D'Amore's writing. I am first and foremost a mother, family woman, restaurateur, mentor and a friend and lover of the Italian community.

Carmela's book is her journey within that Italian environment; of lessons learnt, traditions forgotten, ideas resurrected and the conversations of her heritage that nudge at her heart and soul.

And now, having come full circle as a wife, mother, chef, teacher and tour guide, Carmela has chosen to spread her word with the promise that new generations will love and value it as much as she does.

I have known Carmela for quite a number of years now, in fact, since she published her first book of Sicilian recipes, *Carmela's Cucina Povera*. How refreshing to meet someone so passionate about the foods, the smells and memories of her youth... something all migrants must have felt, including my own mother. It is something that we, as children of migrants, can certainly all identify with.

The commonality was that they all arrived hungry for a new life. However, what kept those early migrants inexplicably connected was, in fact, those memories that they could bring to their everyday lives, fraught with sufferance, loneliness and anticipation but, above all, it was this connection with family that is at the core of Carmela's philosophy.

Let's be frank, with the passing of generations we face the passing of traditions and Carmela is here to keep that torch burning. I mean, how can one explain an aroma wafting through the kitchen in the early hours of the morning, of a mother, any mother, preparing a meal which requires time, patience, knowhow? No Google search can replicate that; it can only give you the black and white facts. It lacks the emotional pill that Carmela keeps enforcing and re-emphasising. She is totally emotive, almost holistic in her writings.

Is there a correlation between food, wine, family, tradition and perhaps we can even include a bit of sexual excitement? I mean, doesn't that image of a glamorous Sofia Loren with an apron on and at the stove embody all that? Her global image pushed all those boundaries of Italianism. She sold style, fashion, beauty, but, most importantly, she sold the story of her roots and she did it proudly, always returning to the heart of her table.

Italy has 20 different regions with 20 different hearts. The north gives us a life that is orderly, refined, more business-like, even perhaps perceived to be more successful as they were brilliant marketers. However, the south gives us colour, heat, wildness, generosity and a Mediterranean lifestyle. Carmela describes this so aptly.

Does a regal Parmigiano-Reggiano in all its northern glory taste any better than a plump blue sardine drowning in that southern extra virgin olive oil with lashings of chilli?

Carmela has romantically captured one of those hearts, that of Sicily and it has taken her a lifetime.

Food evokes emotions and can bring us back to memories in a given moment in time so that we can take it to the heart of the table.. Something that we can take to the very heart can be a jug of wine, such as an Etna Rosso from those volcanic soils, or a Barolo in a heavy fat bottle... neither is better nor worse, it is just what you know, it is the heart of each and every table.

Carmela's writings remind me of the joy at the table: the conversations, comparisons, commentary, arguments, sharing, tastes, smells, traditions... the strength of family which can change in the blink of an eye. When a nonna or a mamma passes, who is going to prepare the baccalà, cure the olives, make the passata? Why didn't I ask more questions? Why didn't I write down the recipes? Carmela reminds us constantly of this. It is one thing to cook, quite another to teach and share with no secrets barred.

When Carmela talks of God's kitchen, she talks of exactly what embodies Italian cuisine... tomato, eggplant, cheese, espresso, etc. Where would food be in this country if it were not for these foundations? Pasta culture, pizza culture, coffee culture... all must have shared some of these ingredients to have taken centre stage. There are usually a thousand versions of the same thing, someone's Bolognese is someone else's Ragù. As I said, this all goes back to the heart of the table and how you remember it.

It has taken Carmela a lifetime to absorb, embrace and tell her story, so sit back, pour yourself a glass of your favourite vino and enjoy her journey.

*Caterina Borsato*
*Restaurateur and lover of all things Italian*

# INTRODUCTION

**Food cooked from the heart creates memories that last a lifetime.**

There is a place in all of us that we call a home. To some people, home is represented by possessions, but my personal treasure is my family, and our kitchen table is the heart of our home.

Life throws us many challenges and we can easily lose our way. Through my own personal experiences, I have learned that the most important elements of life – family, food and our community – will always help us navigate back to where we need to be.

Writing this book has reconnected me with the treasures of my own heart and made me think about how the home functions at its best when everyone is working towards their specific purpose and spending time with each other.

We live in a fast-paced world that is constantly evolving and changing. Somehow, families have lost the ability to communicate well with each other.

*The kitchen table is the heart of the home; it is the centrepiece where love resides.*

Our children rarely play in the street anymore and we all find ourselves more connected to the digital world than with each other. Devices have taken over our families; we have replaced the kitchen table with the television and we wonder why our communication lines are down!

We need to re-direct this attention to our loved ones, to the people who need us to guide them. *The Heart of the Table* is for those who have forgotten what is truly important. This is your answer to the call for help, a guide for the family, for those we can hear the calling of the heart.

If you have picked up this book, please listen to the calling, as I believe it is for you. I have written this book to inspire you, to redirect the dynamics of your family, to give you the motivation to take the steps you have been wanting to take and to call you to your higher purpose.

My Sicilian heritage has taught me that food can heal; it can link you to a forgotten memory and help you find your true self. Food is our teacher, and family and food go well together, don't you think?

Spending time with family and food builds strong and healthy bonds. While I am not a psychologist or a doctor, I am a wife, mother and nonna. I have lived a life where food is at the centre of everything, it is the most important decision we make during the day; what we eat and how we eat.

And in this book, I explore the connection between food and family and how these two components of life gather at the heart of our table.

Take your time to read these pages, let the words resonate with you, read the words, and drink the water, listen to what the voice of truth is expressing, allow yourself the time to reflect. We will share a vision together; it is one of purpose and intention.

These words are for you.

**Carmela Amato D'Amore**

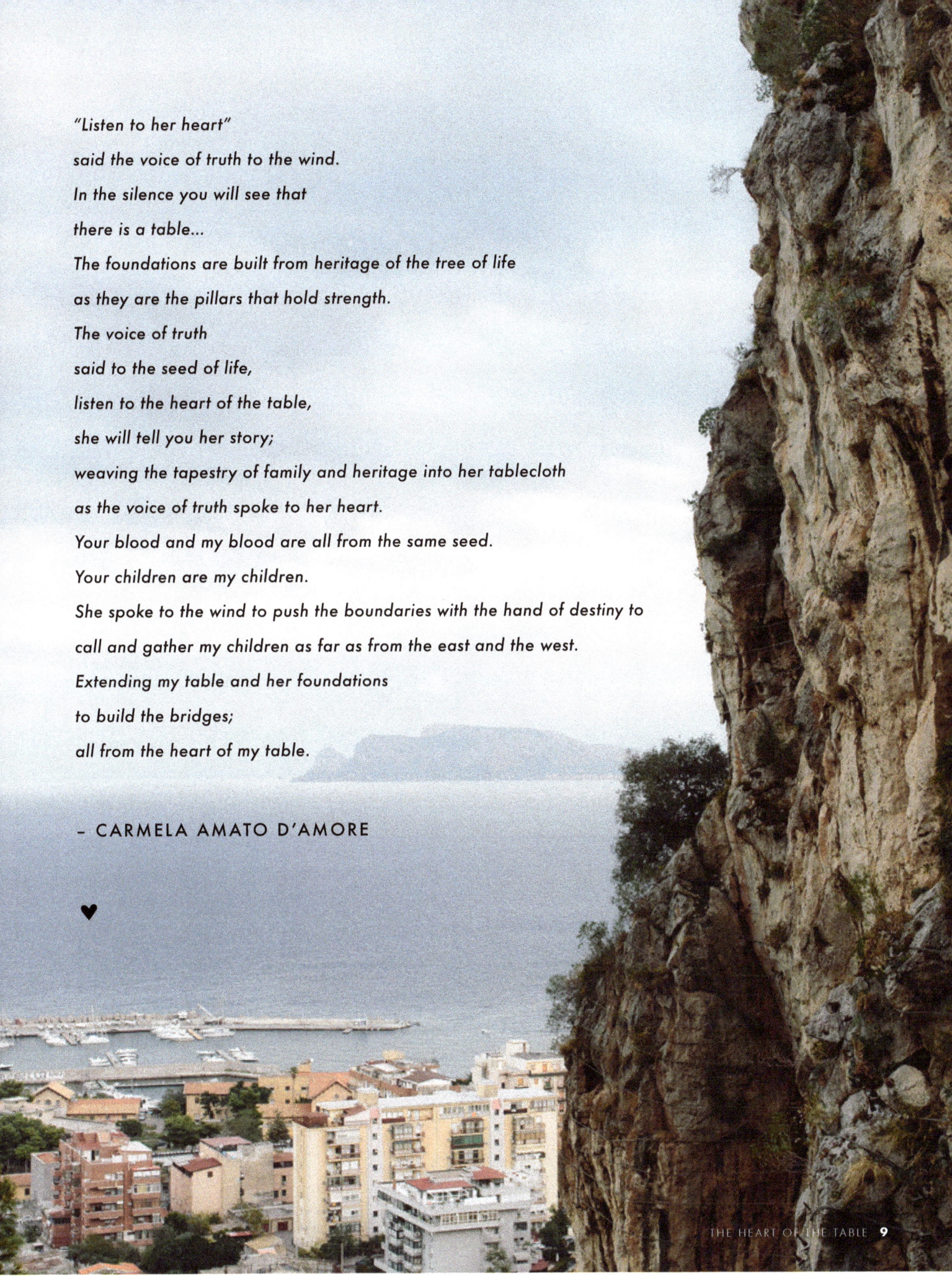

"Listen to her heart"

said the voice of truth to the wind.

In the silence you will see that

there is a table…

The foundations are built from heritage of the tree of life

as they are the pillars that hold strength.

The voice of truth

said to the seed of life,

listen to the heart of the table,

she will tell you her story;

weaving the tapestry of family and heritage into her tablecloth

as the voice of truth spoke to her heart.

Your blood and my blood are all from the same seed.

Your children are my children.

She spoke to the wind to push the boundaries with the hand of destiny to

call and gather my children as far as from the east and the west.

Extending my table and her foundations

to build the bridges;

all from the heart of my table.

— CARMELA AMATO D'AMORE

♥

PART ONE:

# Unlocking the treasure

# CHAPTER 1 – THE WAY

*Heritage is the root of the table. Opening the doors and into my kitchen you come… may grace and the hands of destiny take hold of the sails and change this course.*

There is a knock at my door. Welcome!

I recognise you, dear reader. This is a divine appointment, being in the right place at the right time. I know that together we can unlock the treasure within and find clarity. Come in and take a seat.

I have been wanting to talk to you about so many things that have been concerning me for quite a while, and I needed the timing to be right. I have concerns that are becoming headaches, which have turned into migraines that won't go away. Your face keeps appearing everywhere.

This is the right time for this talk to unravel what is within me. I wonder if you feel the same way. I have decided that it is time to have this chat with you – no texting or glancing at our phones. Instead, we will spend this time creating a law of attraction in our lives. It's important that these words resonate within you. Only then can we move forward and make this change.

## A CHANGE OF SEASON

Every season has its time to share what it has to offer, whether it be spring, winter, summer or autumn. For me, it is the season to write to you and express the things that are concerning me.

My decades of hospitality have shown me many families coming and going, including the evolution of my own family. I have observed the weaving of generations, and following the traditions of families and the community has steered me into the responsibility to share with you my knowledge.

Economies have changed and will continue to change, traditions fade and cultures grow, but *heritage* and *family* will continue to flourish into each generation until the end of time. Growth is part of evolution, we cannot stop it, but we can steer and manage our sails.

Get comfortable and let's share an espresso or a latte. Would you like a biscotto? I make my own, but of course you know that! I love them, they're good for our wellbeing.

Wellbeing – I love this word my dear friend, do you know about wellbeing? Our entire wellbeing is at stake. I don't want to scare you, but we really need to get to the bottom of this conversation otherwise we will begin to chit-chat, and the season will disappear.

## LET'S SLOW IT DOWN

We have entered into a generation of fast food, fast cars, fast sex, fast relationships, fast everything! There is no time for anything, not even sleep. (And we wonder why we can't sleep.)

Can you see it?

I believe that mobile devices have taken control of our young generation and have removed their ability to concentrate and pay attention. These days, it seems we are not able to communicate without these devices.

How can we encourage our children and loved ones to communicate with other people and with us? Do we leave it to society, television or the media to teach them these communication skills?

## THE WEALTHY STATE OF CEMETERIES

I believe that cemeteries are the wealthiest places in the world because they hold so many dreams.

These are places that hold many people who died with their dreams still held inside and their story was never written, the song never sung, the mother who never got to see her children grow up, the children who never got to grow up, the visionaries who had visions from God never got to fulfil their purpose, the dreamer who never got to fulfil the dream, the treasure that was in those people who never got to shine, bright for all to see.

I mention this to you at the beginning of this book to communicate my passion for making the most of life and realising your dreams. It is my intention to take you to the place where we can rediscover your personal treasure.

## WHY ME?

I was born into a family of restaurateurs and I bring those experiences, as well as the skills I have learned from raising four children, to this discussion. I am a nonna, who was raised by my own grandparents, and I come from a large Sicilian immigrant family. I am the person to unlock this in you.

In this book, I want to explore how we can better communicate with one another. Have you ever wondered what is happening with your relationships, such as those with your children, spouse, parents and friends? Relationships are breaking down. It is clear to see through our reality television shows that are all about the 'seven-year itch', people getting married without having met each other, relationship rescues, etc. And, throughout all this, we are living in the 21st century and don't have the proper tools to communicate with each other!

So, how can we fix this? Should we try and learn from the past? Do the answers lie there? Can the seeds of our ancestors' tree be joined and forged with our own?

I would like to tell you a story about my upbringing. Perhaps it will resonate with you.

## LOOKING TO THE PAST

My Nonno Jack used to say that a person is a seed and, as they grow, the seed becomes a tree. The tree needs to be pruned and shaped, otherwise when the tree takes shape, and if it has not been pruned, it's too late; you are left with a disfigured tree. He would then continue to say that we are to shape our trees from a little twig, and our life experiences will shape the form of our tree.

If we are willing to embrace life, the lessons we learn will mould this tree and it will grow accordingly to its purpose and direction. As it continues to be shaped and pruned, the tree will grow without needing any more assistance. Once it finally takes its shape, a great strong tree can then become very fruitful. Every season, it will bear its fruit and will continue to get ready for each season.

I guess my Nonno Jack knew this from his own life experiences and his abundance of fruit showed as he was a man of status, valour, reputation, honour and riches.

The next part of Jack's parable was about the tree's roots, which he referred to as our family. "Consider that we need to fertilise this tree of ours," he would say. "Together, we can do it. As you sit with me and talk to me we are all connected. I believe that food is the nourishment to life and the table is the centrepiece of our families lives."

When my Nonno Jack would tell this story, I was little and could not comprehend the depth of what he was saying. I would laugh at him and Nonna. But as I grew up, my own tree began to take shape and my experiences continued to teach me about who I am in life and, most of all, in my family. With his words, my Nonno had implanted seeds in me that slowly took their shape.

*When you eat, always eat together at the table – this is where the connection lies.*

*Relationships need watering, time, they need to be fertilised and maintained, otherwise they will grow wild.*

## WHO AM I?

**What are our foundations? Who are our mentors today? What are the core values that hold our families together?**

We work all day and come home late, rush to prepare dinner and get ready to start another day.

We think we are working at creating for our family. But we have no time for anything except the things we think are important. In the meantime, however, we create more headaches, cracks in relationships and deeper scars. What happened to the time we used to spend with each other without any distractions?

I remember sitting at the kitchen table with my Nonna and Nonno, and we would talk for hours. In winter we would have the stove going (we did not have central heating).

They would tell me stories of war, famine, love, children, their parents, their families and their words were the warmth to my soul.

*La tavola is the ritual where each generation meets and greets.*

Their faces would light up the kitchen and the table felt like home, the centrepiece of my family. The smells and aromas of cooking and baking made me always feel like home. (Even today, my favourite place is the kitchen.)

## TWO FUNDAMENTAL LIFE CORNERSTONES

There are two fundamental cornerstones in life: relationships and wellbeing. Without relationships, there is no family unity. Relationships are the ties that link, bind and unite us all. Without foundations, we cannot build and create strong relationships.

A relationship is a communion with another being; it is sharing and building a life together. We were born for more than just ordinary lives. It is our role to create the world you want with another, to build a family and weave all of what you have learnt so far, and instill it, into your own family.

Wellbeing research tells us that the touch from one person can transcend into the soul of another and make them well. Are you working towards the best wellbeing for yourself and your family?

We think working with our nose to the grindstone and putting food on the table is the most important function of our lives. Well, for a while it is, but the heart of what matters most is our wellbeing. Without it, we cannot function. We become merely a robot without feelings or warmth. Nothing beats quality, face-to-face time with our family and friends.

*Our families are our ministries; they are the legacy we leave behind.*

The table is where relationships and wellbeing come together. Human touch at the table is more precious than gold.

Sicilian food is all about family, heritage and culture. It is rich with centuries of simple, seasonal food that has taste and gusto. Seasonal produce and eating off the land is the way to genuine wellbeing and health, and that's why Sicilian food is known as God's kitchen.

Wellbeing is based on spirit, mind, body and soul. Without all three, we are not in alignment with our selves.

What we eat today is who we become tomorrow. When we eat healthy food, we think better and live longer lives with the energy to approach every day's events.

Our health, both physical and mental, impacts our relationships. If we only eat fast food and frozen meals, it clogs our brains and we cannot think properly.

## FOOD TEACHES US OUR HISTORY

Food from your heritage teaches you about your life, structure and foundations. Food connects us with our history as though all of our ancestors have sat at the same table.

We have history that speaks to us, of Jesus and the last supper. They all sat with each other and gathered together to discuss the day's events, connect and strengthen their ministry, right? His people are still followers today, centuries later.

We can learn from history. It is up to you and I to take responsibility and learn from our history and make the best for our future. The steering wheel is in our hands. We are the captains of our ship. Will it sink? Will it glide?

Let's not shove this under the tablecloth; let's get clear about how things really are!

We are the co-creators and master planners of this time and era. It is up to us to teach our children about respect, honour, integrity, value and love. These are the principles of the past and we need to steer, direct, spread and sprinkle these seeds into the future generation's hearts and minds.

Our past generations want to talk to us. Can we hear what they are saying? They want us to know about heart, soul, family, food, heritage and the table. It's time to look up and see what direction we are heading and unlock our treasure within. Listen and you will hear.

## QUESTIONS FOR YOU TO REFLECT ON:

*Where do you want to be in life?*

*Where is your family heading?*

*Where do you see yourself in 10 years, 20 years?*

*What legacy do you want to leave behind?*

# CHAPTER 2 – THE HEART OF YOUR SEAT

*Open your heart to the tree of life across the table.*

Circumstances do not make you; they reveal where you are, nudge you in the moment and direct you to the place you are meant to be.

I want to tell you a story. It is a true story about a man living in America in the early 1920s. He was very wealthy and he used all of his money to invest in a property.

He believed that there was wealth in the land. But once he started digging into it, he noticed lots of black rocks just beneath the ground's surface, all over his property. He dug up the land and continued to discover these black rocks. He knew nothing about them and found them very frustrating, as he had to spend all of his money digging up the land.

It wasn't long until he used up all of his resources and finally, after decades of digging and not getting anywhere, he became depressed and gave up. Sadly, he took his own life and the property was taken by the state. A local man purchased the property and he soon began digging the land to find these black rocks all over.

But rather than give up, he did something that no one had ever thought of – he went to the local library to investigate and research these rocks and was diligent at finding the resolution. Do you know what happened?

He discovered that he was living on a diamond field – the black rocks were diamonds! He was living on so much wealth and became extremely wealthy. He did what most people don't even think about. He educated himself and was rewarded for doing so.

I believe that we are all living on a diamond field. It is our family who makes us rich; they are our diamonds, our legacy we leave behind. It takes hard work to understand our family and we need to be persistent and educate ourselves, to never stop trying to understand our family – what a personal treasure our families are – it takes work to make it shine.

## DNA

What is DNA? DNA is a long molecule that contains our unique genetic code. A single gene may be many thousands of bases long. Each cell contains two sets of genes, one from your mother and one from your father.

And just from that you were born! You were created. You exist.

You were chosen to live a life and give life, if possible. Be part of an evolution of people and contribute your gifts to this earth. This is your seat at the table and your life – right here, right now.

From this life that has chosen you, you begin to take shape and learn from your parents, friends, family and people that are part of your world. You are like a sponge ready to take shape and grow from what you have learnt.

We, as people, are the result of a compound full of treasure from each of our ancestors, and it all lies within us. As you take shape, you develop a spirit, personality, character and voice. Throughout this journey, your family remains connected to you and grows with you.

## A SHOUT-OUT TO THE MEN OF THE FAMILY

*A father is the first hero of a son and the first love of a daughter.*

I want to take a moment to give a shout out to the men of the family, as you are all of our heroes.

In our family, you are the compass of our course and without your direction, we would be like dust in the wind. The men in our lives are the first people to speak life into us; they are the ones who mould and shape us. You are our leaders, our mentors, our coaches, and your words direct our sails and enforce the strength in our lives.

Your voice is our teacher and the leader we so desperately need. Do not ever underestimate how much we value you in our lives. We will not get lost with your voice to guide us. Your seat is the most important and powerful one.

The depth of your family is you; you are the roots as we come from your seeds.

Your voice comforts us when you say "it's okay." I have seen fathers and grandfathers who can quieten a baby from crying, just by speaking to them. It is certainly true from seeing my nonno, father, husband and sons with their children.

*Biology means nothing – a father is one who is there for you, who loves you and always wants the best for you.* ♥

You are the king of value, strength, honour, integrity. You are the lion full of courage; you direct this family that is yours. You are the high potency for your children. You are the stability that strengthens the seed of each one of your family members. Your steadfastness endures for generations to come.

## DAUGHTER'S EYES

*In my father's eyes*

*I am the prize*

*even before he heard my cries.*

*Deep within I reside*

*My past and present*

*are designing my future.*

*In the treasure of your heart*

*lies the seeds of my tree.*

*From the mystery of this one event,*

*I become the present.*

*From your courage and hope,*

*you have forged my path.*

*Your love reflects*

*my treasure within.*

*Value and respect*

*is the reflection in your eyes.*

*And in this,*

*I am the prize.*

## A SHOUT-OUT TO THE WOMEN OF THE FAMILY

There is so much I want to tell you about being a grandmother. It is the most rewarding role, it is like stepping into grace. Being a mother was tough – I had to take care of everything while trying to enjoy the moments.

Being a grandmother and nonna is the best role in the family. You get to enjoy your grandchildren and then give them back but, in the meantime, the lessons you learnt along the way are the ones you teach to your grandchildren.

A mother (mamma) is diligent. She is the person who is there for every event in your life, there to take you wherever you need to go and is there to cook, clean and do everything to run the household. In today's modern world, this is also a father's job! A mamma loves you when you are sick. She is the person who gives you the blessing when it's your time to leave; she makes sure that you have everything you need. Your mamma plays a major role in your life.

(For those who are not fortunate to have a mother or grandmother in your life, I hope that you have a woman of calibre to help steer your journey.) An auntie or female friend could have raised you. I have seen sisters raise their siblings very well, especially in Italian families.

Can you visualise each person at the table? The table needs all of your relatives in each place for you to have the best dynamic.

*A Nonna is a mentor. She is the person who loves you unconditionally. She sees the past and present in you and loves you more than you will ever know until you become her.* ♥

### GRANDPARENTS DAY IN ITALY

Italy has celebrated Grandparents Day, which they call *Buona Festa dei Nonni*, since 2005. It is celebrated on 2 October – a date when Catholics also celebrate guardian angels. On this day, grandparents are invited to schools and they are honoured and 'feasted'.

The children often sing a song called 'Thou Shalt' on this day. 'Ninna Nonna' is another popular song that is considered the unofficial song of Grandparents Day. An annual prize, the *Il Premio nazionale del nonno e della nonna d'Italia*, is given annually to grandparents who have distinguished themselves with meritorious service.

I want to mention Grandparents Day here because Italian and Sicilian grandparents are honoured to be grandparents. They are constant givers and generous with their families and they present a good example of how we should all strive to be.

The root of our family, the older generations, are what connects us to the past. Our destinies are tied at the table.

### BE THE BEST VERSION OF YOU

Your seat at the table is just as important as everyone else's. Life without you would not be possible. It's imperative that you understand how important you are.

Your heart is what beats and makes this seat important, you might not realise this now, but you will understand that without you it's not possible for your family to be whole.

Without your face across the table, it would not be the same. Your words are the seeds that will shape your family. Your life will move towards the power of your words.

Choose your words, as they are the shaping force that will direct the sails of your family. This will enable you to pass the right guidance to the next generation.

---

### WISE SAYINGS ABOUT WOMEN ♥

*Quando una madre è nata entra in grazia.*
When a mother is born she steps into grace.

*Amore di Madre, amore senza limiti.*
A mother's love has no limits.

*L'affetto verso i genitori e fondamento di ogni virtu.* Loving one's parents is fundamentally the greatest virtue.

*Una buona mamma vale cento maestre.*
A good mother is worth a hundred teachers.

*Se non sta andando bene, chiamate la nonna.* If nothing is going well, call your grandmother.

## FIVE LIFE LESSONS

Throughout my life, I have grown to understand that certain life lessons are more important than others. Here they are.

### Lesson one: your choices affect everything

The choices you make affect everyone around you, and you are pretty powerful among your clan. Your power influences and directs, even if you just have a little voice. Your voice is connected through this spiritual cord. Do you believe it?

### Lesson two: the power is in your belief system

Your belief system is the essence of your structure. In that structure is everything that you believe and your world is created and always influenced by your belief system.

There is a well-known proverb that says, "as a man believes, so is he." Your ability to believe is the key. You must believe in who you are and what you have come here for to continue your purpose. Be strong in your beliefs as your family is listening, and being influenced, by everything you do and say.

### Lesson three: put your heart into whatever you do

The most important thing in life is what is in your heart as this will shape where your actions are coming from, how you influence and how you manage your family. Are you a motivator or an inspiration? You and your intention shapes your family.

The second most powerful thing is to believe in what you do. If you conduct your life from a place of love and generosity, watch how your life unfolds.

### Lesson four: your seat is powerful, especially at the table

Your words are gospel; they are the breath of life, they give life to the weary, they are the creation. As God spoke, he created the world.

Words are powerful; they can break or shape a human. When I was growing up we had a saying, "sticks and stones may break your bones but words can never hurt me." This saying is so untrue.

You are the creator of your family; your words are like water in the desert. They are the stars in the night. Words are the oxygen in your air; they are the foundation of your very existence. Words can change a thought pattern and direct you towards victory.

### Lesson five: build the power of your seat at the table

It is so important to believe in yourself. You need to be empowered to be able to be strong for yourself and your family. You are unique and we need you.

Through diligence, perseverance and discipline you will build the power of your seat at the table, and your words will be the fuel that ignites the passion of your family. Through life's trials and obstacles, you need to believe in the 'we' and the 'us' of the family, there is no I.

This is where the strength lies: in your home and community. There will be times when the storms of life will hit you. If you have prepared for this and built a strong and powerful fortress, you will not be shaken and you will stand stronger.

## THOUGHT-PROVOKING QUESTIONS

To get at the core of my purpose, I have asked myself the following questions many times throughout my life. These questions act as a trigger to activate the direction of your life.

### Q: Who am I?

This is the most profound question that I have asked myself. It took me a long time to answer, but it was always there in the back of my mind. It was the most liberating question when I truly found the answer.

### Q: Where am I from?

You will never know who you are if you don't know where you came from. Your heritage is the pinnacle of you.

### Q: Why am I here?

You could follow this question up with: why was I conceived? Why was I born? Have you ever asked yourself those questions? When you find the answers to the purpose of your life, it is the door to freedom. It may take you all your life to answer but these are very important questions. As you find your purpose, you will be able to direct your family into higher dimensions.

### Q: What are my talents and skills?

This question involves figuring out what you can do with your life to create meaning. Answering this question is a life-long challenge. It is all about discovering the core to your passion.

### Q: Where am I going?

I love this question. There is a proverb in the bible that says, "A man without a vision will perish." Having no plan for your life is like being blind; you lose sight of where you are going.

## AWAKEN THE ATTITUDE OF GRATITUDE

To discover what is truly in my heart, I use a gratitude journal. Writing down what I am grateful for in life creates an attitude of gratefulness. This exercise creates a pattern in your mindset that reinforces new beliefs and a closer connection with your heart.

Let's practise this together. I'll help you through it. First, write down the name of a family member who shares your table. Close your eyes and take a deep breath. Then, follow these steps:

- Dwell in a state of gratitude
- Remember a time that you felt grateful
- Put both hands on your heart and feel its beat
- Take some more deep breaths
- Visualise a family member
- Think about how grateful you are for them
- Think about how life would not be the same without them
- Think about how that person makes your life so much better by being in it
- Remain aware of your heartbeat
- Stay in this moment, it will follow you all day.

Repeat this exercise every morning and evening. Do this with each family member and your heart will be so full of love for each person. When you are sharing the table together, remember that feeling and stay in that energy, you will be surprised by the energy it gives you at the table. It will create a spirit of unity and family.

For those of you who do not yet have children, think about how grateful you will be when they arrive – visualise them in your life. This creates a path for your future.

**Use this space to write down what you are grateful for today:**

..................................................................

..................................................................

..................................................................

..................................................................

..................................................................

..................................................................

# CHAPTER 3 – THE SPIRIT OF FAMILY

*Your journey leads you home.*

I come from the generation where we fix what is broken, we don't throw it away. Our modern world isn't broken, there is just a crack in it. We have forgotten what is important. We have lost our way. Through my words, I hope to lead you to the path of what life truly is about.

My entire Amato family (including grandparents) immigrated to Australia in the early 1950s from the backdraft of World War II. Growing up in the 1960s was amazing. We had *festa* (a celebration) every week, especially at my parents' house because they had a big garage. All of my aunties, uncles, cousins, *compare's*, *commare's* and friends would get together and we would create one long table in the garage.

Everyone would be cooking or bring food and we had so much fun together, laughing and connecting. This created strong family ties which lasted for a generation. The next generation of children unfortunately didn't have such strong ties.

## CONNECTING THROUGH FOOD

During the week, my parents and grandparents would create food that was from their homeland and I could see that they were connecting with their home through the food.

They had brought only a suitcase with them to Australia, but when they ate they connected with home. This spirit continued for many years and into the next generation. But, pretty soon, the future generation was born and the tie was not as strong.

*Food from the soul opens the door to the heart's appetite.* ♥

This was not just my family. In the 1960s, there were so many families that helped shape what Australia is today as it was the economic boom of building the family structure. Australia is a multicultural society and each ethnicity had their own way of connecting to culture through food.

Australian families got together every Sunday with a delicious roast dinner. I would drool over my friends' roast dinners, they smelt divine! You could smell the chicken or lamb cooking right into the street. No-one cooked spuds like the Aussie grandmother, they were just perfect!

Greek families gathered together to roast meat (usually lamb) on the spit. You could smell the garlic, oregano and rosemary and hear their Greek music blaring loudly throughout the neighbourhood.

Jewish families would gather together for their Sabbath dinner and still today continue with this way of life. The Sabbath is communing with God and family, being thankful for everything.

It remains today that multitudes of multicultural families have their own rituals of gathering together at their table.

Going back to that crack, it's there to guide us and show us how to repair and strengthen our families and their future. Fast food, and even fast eating, creates bad habits, health issues, mental issues and isolation in families.

Can we learn from the past? Most certainly. We need to bring the spirit of family into this new millennium. It is up to us to share our history, recreate strong family ties and build a future around what the table truly represents in our family.

## 10 WAYS TO BUILD THE TREASURES OF YOUR FAMILY

### 1. Create family rituals that will empower your entire family

Words are the creative life force of your sails. When you speak, you create steering words of encouragement and building for your family. Create a ritual where you encourage the children in your family when they achieve something. Always speak encouraging words to your family.

### 2. Be there

Your kids regard your presence as a sign of care, connection, communication, collaboration and communing. It's crucial for you to spend as much time as possible with them. Create space where you are available. Spending time together will lay the groundwork for the seeds of your family to grow.

### 3. Express affirmation, warmth and encouragement

Parents who practise loving parenting, as opposed to shame-based parenting, will create a home where children and spouses feel more secure and their relationships will grow. For example, encouraging your family with words such as "you are amazing", "how wonderful are you", etc. plants seeds of confidence in this young budding being.

### 4. Build healthy morals and values

The choices that our children make today will affect them for the rest of their lives. Study their culture so that you can understand what cultural influences currently pose a danger to your child's spirit. Get to know what your children are watching on TV and in the movies.

Watch and listen to the media together as often as possible and talk with them about what you are watching. By doing this, you will learn how they observe the world.

### 5. Discipline with consistency

When you clearly express your expectations and consistently follow through, you'll produce responsible children. Keep in mind that consistent discipline takes lots of time and energy. However, diligence and persistence will benefit you in the long term.

### 6. Ruthlessly eliminate stress

A busy and unbalanced life will not be kind to the areas that we neglect; it is like a garden without the gardener. Get some form of guidance to help you decide which activities to eliminate from your family's schedule if you're too busy to get enough rest and free time every day and evening.

Don't neglect spending lots of time with your family for anything, including your career. Make whatever sacrifices you need to make so you can enjoy plenty of relaxed family time together.

### 7. Communicate well

Positive communication is the language of love for your children. Make a habit of listening carefully to your children whenever they share their thoughts and feelings with you. Also, figure out how to best express your love for your kids in ways that each of them will receive well. Apologise to them when you've made a parenting mistake.

Allow the conflicts you experience with your spouse and kids to be a path to deeper communication by helping you all understand each other better and work as a team to solve problems.

### 8. Play together

There is nothing like play to bring about family togetherness and tenderness. Make time for family vacations, have fun at home, go on frequent outings (from going out for ice cream to taking music or sports lessons together), share holiday traditions, enjoy humour together and work on projects together. Sharing playful experiences will build family memories that will bond you all in powerful ways.

### 9. Love your spouse

If you're married or have a partner, cultivate the soil in your relationship regularly and invest in it by going on frequent dates. A loving relationship brings hope and security to your kids and it strengthens the treasure within them.

If you're a single parent, build relationships with friends at your child's school and in groups with people who genuinely care about your children and are willing to invest in their lives. Build relationships with your children's grandparents. They will be able to support and assist you in difficult times.

Marriage is a union of souls, a spiritual partnership, a shared union to enhance the vision of your family and it is a commitment to your family.

### 10. Remember that the best things in life aren't things

Managing the finances is an important part of the energy flow in any family. Follow a budget to live below your means, avoid debt, give in other generous ways and save regularly.

Modelling these healthy financial practices will teach your children valuable practical and spiritual lessons. Children don't really understand what is important; it is you, the parent, who is the guardian and mentor.

## HOW TO ENERGISE YOUR FAMILY'S SPIRITUAL GROWTH

Your greatest calling in life is to leave a spiritual legacy for your children. Your relationship with your family is equivalent to one with God. It involves having faith that there is a higher power that is more than us; it's like getting up in the morning and believing in things that have not even happened yet. As you grow, so will your children - their faith, love, joy, patience and steadfastness.

When you pray for and with your children, you show them that there is more to life than what they see. Start by saying little prayers with them and you will see that they will take charge and believe as their faith is stronger than adults. It's a good idea to write a family declaration that describes your family's values.

> ### EXAMPLE: A FAMILY DECLARATION
>
> I declare that my family will experience God's faithfulness. I will not doubt. I will keep my trust in Him to give birth to every promise put in my heart and I will become everything that God created me to be.
>
> I declare a firewall of protection for my family. I declare God's incredible blessing over my family, and I will see an explosion of God's goodness. I will experience the surpassing greatness of God's favour in my life and family.
>
> Amen and it will be so.

For those who have no belief in God, there is intelligence in this universe that surpasses our own human intelligence. It is called faith in the unseen. We all believe that we will wake up tomorrow. It is your faith that requires the action.

Remember that this is your ministry, your family, your treasure - this is what you have invested in and it will be the reward of your future. You are investing in your future assets. What better way to start this ministry than at your table?

Ask your family or loved ones what kind of rituals they would like to see at the table. You can make up your own as you go, there are no rules in life, you make them up as you go. Work with what suits you. Love is the key to guide you.

Inspiration comes from the word in spirit – divine influence, an action or power of moving intellect or emotions. When we inspire others, fuel and water fills God's Holy Spirit into the other person, and through those actions we also empower our own spirit – it is like water to the seed of the soul.

## FAMILY

*Il mondo senza famiglia è come la luna senza le stelle.* The world without family is like the moon without the stars.

Have you ever been woken up in the middle of the night and gone outside and looked up at the stars in the sky? There are so many wonderful and beautifully shaped stars, and they all shine bright. To me, this represents family – we are all different and so unique and wonderfully made.

Italian families stick together through thick and thin. It's not uncommon for extended families to live together, even after the children are married with families of their own. To us, family is an integral part of everyday life.

My entire life has been built around my family. Each member grows with you through your whole life. If you have been blessed to have your mamma and papa then you all evolve together.

In some cultures, family represents wealth, richness and immortality. In other cultures, family is what they work and live for. There are different types of families – people who are married, separated, biologically related, adopted, blended families, families with one parent, the list goes on.

My intention is to navigate you into the direction of building a great family. My vision for you is to open up the heart of your table.

*La famiglia viene prima – the family comes first. These words are concrete evidence of what is truth. Family is the glue that binds us together.*

### MY FAMILY DECLARATION

I declare a legacy of faith and hope over my family. I declare that I will store up blessings for the future generations. My life is forged by experience and integrity. Through making the right choices and takings steps of faith, God's abundance is surrounding my family today.

My family is unique and different. We are like the stars in the night, held by love and we will forge our way through faith and love. Amen, it will be so.

All families are different; there is none like the other. That's what makes families unique.

The family structure is one that is up to us to decide. Whichever way it works, as long as it is for the good of all, that's the most important.

Each family member is diverse and yet all are linked through blood or family ties. Blended families or step-families are just as strong as blood; it is the history that holds them together.

As we have the seasons in life, so do we have the same with family. Sometimes when it's summer you just want to have fun together and when it's spring you have picnics and enjoy each other's company. When it's autumn, you reflect on the gratitude you have for each other and winter is a time to rekindle your ties and enjoying staying at home with each other. There is growth in all seasons.

Let your home be the sanctuary of the family.

# CHAPTER 4 – EVERY TABLE TELLS A STORY

*Breathe life into the story of your table.*

My mission is to create a new platform that combines food and conversation to open up the communication lines, so that people can collaborate with one other once again.

## LA TONNARA DI MILAZZO

I want to share a family story with you. I love telling this story as it created the story of my own table. It is the very platform that I have built my family on.

My mother Sarina's father, Nonno Stefano, was a tuna fisherman. He was the last engineer of the bay of Il Tonno di Milazzo. At the end of the fishing season, all the women from the village would cook up a huge feast; through the evening and well into the morning.

During mid-morning, all the men and children would carry their dining tables out onto the street to create one long table. When the food was ready, each woman having cooked a dish from her own kitchen, they would put the food on the table and everyone in the community would eat and celebrate the end of the tuna season.

*It created a strong sense of community and family that spread all the way into the town. Everyone knew each other and, as a result, the community was tight knit.*

How amazing is that? Everyone sitting and enjoying the food and it would go for hours into the evening.

This is a story that has followed me from four generations ago. My mother Sarina would tell me this story of her father and growing up I got to witness it myself. This is the start of the story of my table.

The values of this story come down to embracing family, the community and extending our tables. We do not live in that kind of environment anymore, but that does not mean that we cannot change, one table at a time, through extending it into our families' lives and the community.

Let's do some thinking together. I have added reflection questions below to get you thinking and challenge your old beliefs and mindset. You can shift away from your old way of thinking through your behaviour, but let's start by considering these questions.

## QUESTIONS TO REFLECT ON

*Is there a time that you can remember when you sat at the table in your childhood and felt at home?*

*What do all of your family members represent to you?*

*How can you continue the spirit of family into the next generation?*

*Where do you want to lead your family?*

*How do you want to be remembered by your family?*

Prayers are the water that makes our faith grow. Together with hope, prayers can create a lifetime of blessings and by declaring things into existence, with one spoken word, we call out to the universe and our faith grows from our belief. These beliefs are the seeds that our children need to see and hear as it shows them something outside of their own world view. When we believe, it creates a better perception and provides clarity; it creates a community-centred heart.

### BLESSINGS FOR MY TABLE

I declare unexpected blessings are coming my way. I will move forward from barely making it to having more than enough. God will open up supernatural doors for me and my family. He will speak to the right people about me, and I will see increases in my life. Amen.

God's dream for my family is coming to pass; it will not be stopped by people, disappointments or adversities. God has solutions to every problem I will face already lined up. The right people and the right breaks are coming in my future and I will fulfil my destiny.

I declare God's blessing on my family and the table I share. When you change the way you look at things, the things you look at change. I declare that the grace of God touches each and every member of my family and may it extend into everyone that I touch. ♥

## LAYING THE GROUNDWORK

Together we have laid the groundwork and our intentions to create a better connection with our family. Now, we will build the structure to create strength. We need to look up sometimes and figure out what direction we are going in. Sometimes we can get so busy working that we forget how beautiful life really is.

Each member of the family is unique and wonderfully made. They already come with their own personalities; they have a purpose in life and it's up to us to steer them in the right direction in their life. Each family member has their own story that will unfold as they proceed through their journey.

When you think of your family, all sitting around your table, what do you see? What story does it tell you? When you think of this, do you feel grateful for your blessings?

We have the chance to create the best day every day, as long as we approach life with the attitude of gratitude.

*Creating a family is the most rewarding and unique experience we can give to the world.*

Visualise the word 'grateful' and say it slowly in your mind and out loud. Meditate on this word to create the best day possible.

Grateful. The Latin word gratus, meaning, 'pleasing' or 'thankful' gives us the root grat. Words from the Latin gratus have something to do with being pleasing or being thankful, feeling or showing an appreciation for something done or received.

Gratefulness is like a tree. It has so many branches – love, joy, happiness, excitement, gentleness, kindness and appreciation.

When you have a child who is continually grateful for everything they have, you automatically want to give them more, don't you? In contrast, when you have a child who is ungrateful, you don't want to be generous with them as you know that they will not appreciate it. An ungrateful attitude blocks their own happiness because you know that they will not be happy with what you give them. So, the more grateful you are, the more you have.

# CHAPTER 5 – A MERE MOTHER; AN IMMIGRANT'S DAUGHTER

*Destiny and purpose direct the course of my table.*

My family came to Australia after World War II to build a better life. They had a vision of creating a future for their children. I have so much admiration and gratitude for their decision to migrate to Australia as the future of my life and that of my children has been steered and shaped by their decision.

I am an immigrant's daughter. Australia is my home; one that I did not choose but was chosen for me. My family gave up their homeland to come to a country that adopted them and they took on a new way of life.

*Immigration. The international movement of people into a destination country of which they are not natives or where they do not possess citizenship in order to settle or reside there.*

## MY MOTHER'S STORY

As she stared into the cold night, there was a distant light coming through the crack of the door. She was deep in thought about the life that was in front of her. What had possessed her to board this ship? This was a pivotal moment; the decision would change the course of her entire life and maybe that of the future lives of others.

The night air was echoing the words of a land that she called home and another was the land filled with promise and hope. She had reached the intersection of her life and she reflected on the events that led her to this moment. Had she dreamt too big this time? What lay before her? She could not even speak English! Had her impulsive behaviour taken her too far?

She had heard the call of many people who were migrating to Australia. But it was a visit from Donna Carmela (who was the first person to call her Sarina) that changed the course of her life. Donna Carmela had left for Australia and her experience was ingrained in her memory. It would not give her rest, she dreamt of nothing else but to come to Australia. She had reached the point of no return and got enough courage to make a decision and told her father and mother of her plans.

She thought about her father, Stefano, for a moment. The sewing machine, which was being held at the bottom of the ship, was his gift to her. It cost him more than he could afford but he wanted her to have it so that she could have a trade to bring to Australia. It gave him solace to know that his little Sara was going to be okay in a country that was unknown to him.

She remembered his tears as she told him she was going to Australia and her mother cried for days. They are a tight-knit family and just the thought of being detached set the emotions rising. She felt a lump rising in her throat and gently wiped away the tears that had surfaced. She took a deep breath.

It was generally unheard of for a single woman to leave her country and set sail across the world! She left all that she knew behind – her five loving sisters, two adoring brothers and all of her friends in her hometown. But Sarina knew that she had a purpose and a destiny.

## FACING HER FEARS

During that month at sea, Sarina faced many of her doubts. Her sole focus was to find a job. She felt safe because Donna Carmela's son, Salvatore, was going to meet her and she had a place to stay with his family.

The home Semi, this is the name everyone called Salvatore, and his brothers, Nunzio and Giuseppe, had bought together was quite small but it offered a place for family and friends to stay while they found jobs and could make enough money to put a deposit on their own home. Over the years, their home in Kensington housed an enormous amount of families and friends who emigrated from Sicily to Australia.

Sarina always had a smile when she thought of Salvatore. His courage and determination to leave their hometown

of Falcone in Sicily was enough to fuel her own fire to approach a promising future. He had a charisma that set him apart.

Semi worked with his brothers and his father, Gioaccino, and they made enough money each day from their fishing boat. However, it was not enough to make a future living.

## IDEAS THAT BECAME REALITY

Sarina arrived to Australia in 1955 at the Princess Pier in Port Melbourne. It had been a voyage of anticipation and a journey of self-examination and she felt great joy seeing Semi and his brothers when she arrived.

Waiting to disembark the ship, her dreams were now becoming a reality. She could now intently pursue her passion for sewing and cooking in Australia.

Gioaccino took Sarina to a Jewish lady named Mrs Gallo as he had heard she was hiring. Later, Sarina worked for Fletcher Jones in Brunswick where she helped employ many friends and family. The sewing machine that Sarina's father had given her increased her expertise and she created many dresses for Mrs Gallo, often working well into the night.

Her employment helped her practise speaking English and Sarina soon felt comfortable with the language. At her job, she interacted with people from many different cultures and her passion and courage for life made this easy. Sarina and Semi married on 25 August 1956 and spent the rest of their lives living on the Mornington Peninsula. They felt at home by the sea.

Can you see where the course of Sarina's life changed? It was crucial to bring a trade with her to shape this new Australia. Her future was already shaped and she made the move to Australia at a good time. It was perfectly aligned for her journey.

I am an immigrant's daughter and I am proud of my heritage. I am also proud that I have a blended identity – I am both Australian and Sicilian. What is your heritage? Have you ever asked your elders what your family lineage is? This is essential as your heritage is the essence of you.

*Write down some of your family's legacy here. What do you remember being told about your heritage?*

..................................................................
..................................................................
..................................................................
..................................................................
..................................................................
..................................................................
..................................................................
..................................................................
..................................................................
..................................................................
..................................................................
..................................................................
..................................................................
..................................................................
..................................................................
..................................................................
..................................................................
..................................................................
..................................................................
..................................................................

# CHAPTER 6 – IS THE TABLE A FADING TRADITION?

*Will the table end as just a fable?*

We are living in an ever-changing world that is constantly evolving. Can tradition continue in this new, fast-paced age? Should we lead by example? Or do we give up? The tradition of gathering around the table with those we love will not vanish if we continue to practise it. We are the caretakers of this tradition. Listen to the heart of the table and use it to shape a life that you call home.

When making our meals, gently and lovingly create a spirit of family around the table. For the table creates a platform for each family member to build his or her own family in the future.

> *We are the ones who must forge the heart of the table with the next generation through truth, perseverance, courage and sheer determination.*

## THE ART OF COOKING

*In this story we all play a part. The love for Sicilian cooking comes straight from my heart.*

Cooking is a skill that we acquire in life and, just like any skill, the more we work on it the better we become. Have you ever become stuck and not known what to cook? Or do you feel like you are always cooking the same meals?

The more we practise cooking and taste our food, we open up our palates and get to enjoy the delicious flavours they bring to our plates. Just like anything in life, when we introduce something new, it takes time for it develop and see where it belongs.

> *Eating seasonal food does not weigh you down; it feeds your soul.*

The seasons are there to teach us about slow food, light food, nurturing food, delicious food and healthy food.

When we eat fast food, we get weighed down because it only fills the hole but it does not satisfy our hunger or wellbeing. Eating healthy food gives us zest for life and enables us to wake up in the morning and feel great, paving the way for a great day.

It is important to introduce new flavours to your cooking each season. Make this a habit and you will find that your palate expands a lot over time.

### Questions for you to reflect on:

*What are you eating? Is it in season?*

*Does your food make you feel great?*

*Do you feel energised after cooking or weighed down with burdens?*

## FREQUENTLY ASKED QUESTIONS

As a chef, I am often asked similar questions by people about food, cooking and how to develop a well-balanced palate. Here are some of my answers to those frequently asked questions.

**Q: How do you know what taste your palate is wanting?**

You must be in tune with your tastebuds to know what your body requires. Look at the food that is in season and use the freshest ingredients you can – this will ultimately create dishes that feed your soul. Our tastebuds are like a muscle, if we don't use them we will lose the flavour that they bring to our senses.

**Q: How do I get my palate going?**

You can introduce new tastes to your palate by cooking with ingredients that are in season. When we eat what is in season, our taste opens up to the produce and we get the most nutrients and flavour from each ingredient.

**Q: How do I get out of a cooking rut?**

If you are feeling stuck and don't have any ideas of new recipes to cook, look for inspiration from other people. Push yourself to keep learning from those who have come before us. You can find a recipe that you like and tweak it to your own palate, using the ingredients that you want.

Dig into old cookbooks or use Google to look for inspiration. Purchase new cookbooks, sign up for a cooking class. Better still, travel! Go somewhere that you have never been before as this is a great way to change your perspective and open up the artist in you.

**Q: I have lost the joy of cooking. How do I get it back?**

Cooking for other people, and using food to inspire those around you, is the biggest motivator to get back in the kitchen and reignite your passion for cooking. Introducing new ingredients into your favourite recipes will also jolt your tastebuds and make you feel happy again.

**Q: Do you have any advice for your fellow chefs?**

Cooking is life; food is medicine; live to enjoy your life and radiate the brilliance of your treasure and bring it to your table.

**PART TWO:**
# The Ingredients of the Table

## LA TAVOLA (THE TABLE)

To tell you where it all began,
there is a story that is so grand.
The one of family and heritage
we all share a part of these ingredients.

Sharing a hand in this plan,
spreading love across the land.
Each sharing from this table,
will it end as just a fable?

There is this table so totally bare;
it is the place that we all get to share.
Am I the storyteller in this life?
Setting the table and preparing like a wife?
I ponder about each person
while lovingly I prepare and chop with my knife.

As the day slowly unfolds,
I get a glimpse of the sunshine with its gold,
greeting me through my windowsill.
All I really want is to sit and be still.

So I need to prepare
as the morning is rare.
All I want to create
is the food on this plate.

In this story, we all have a part;
the love for Sicilian cooking
coming straight from my heart.
It starts with the seed of love to grow
Family and heritage is all that we know.

This table is made of aging wood
And with the times, it has withstood.
It even has become part of this virtual world
just like our pasta that is twirled.

I want to leave a mark;
for this I need a place to spark.
Carmela's Cucina is the place
where Napoli is the base
and family and heritage
are the core ingredients.

There is a song I want to sing
Food and wine are what I bring.

# CHAPTER 7 – THE LEGS OF THE TABLE

*Education begins at the table.*

Everything in life has a recipe and each recipe requires the necessary ingredients to create something wonderful. Just as our cars need proper fuel to run efficiently, our tables need key ingredients to create a table that will last for generations to come.

The legs of our table are the foundations that we build our table from; without legs, where do we stand? And how can we guide and direct our family?

## COMMUNICATION

Communication is crucial to our relationships. Without it, I cannot tell you what I want and I cannot hear you; if there is no open dialogue we cannot hear one another. When we communicate properly with one another, we are on the same page, and even though we are different people, we still understand each other. With proper communication comes respect – we feel free to be our unique selves, which allows us to expand and grow.

Communication skills are the ability to convey or share ideas and feelings effectively. Communication is the imparting or exchanging of information through speaking, writing or using some other medium. Most communication is oral, with one party speaking and others listening. A mixed message occurs when a person's words communicate one message while, non-verbally, he or she is communicating something else.

At the table, communicating is like breathing fresh air. Sitting outside in the sun and enjoying a lovely meal together is like re-fuelling the soul. Verbal communication is gold; it is our trump card to building relationships and it creates a pathway of energy that will flow consistently throughout our entire life.

So, how do we communicate?

The table is the ideal place for a family to communicate. This is a space where we all sit down and have a place to share; we are like shareholders of this space as we have invested our time to be here, and how we choose to communicate is entirely up to each person.

Meeting a family member in a place where they are able to communicate is the key to having a successful relationship; we cannot assume that they have had the same experiences as us. It's like mediation, where all judgments are left aside for the benefit of the cause. In this case, for the family.

*Conversation. A talk, especially an informal one, between two or more people in which news and ideas are exchanged.*

## FIVE WAYS TO INITIATE COMMUNICATION

1. Share a story from your childhood. Opening up relaxes everyone and allows for people to enter into your world.

2. Ask a family member to tell you about a special time in their life that they would like to share.

3. Take an interest in that person's everyday life. Simply ask them "how was your day today?"

4. Offer help. If someone is going through a tough time, ask whether there is anything you can do to help them.

5. Speak words of love and encouragement, such as "I am so blessed to have you in my life."

The ability to communicate information accurately, clearly and as intended is a vital life skill and something that should not be overlooked. This includes your non-verbal communication, such as your body language, eye contact, hand gestures and tone of voice.

It is also important to be a good listener. Communication is about leaving all judgments, thoughts and concerns aside and allowing a person the time to speak and meet you in a holy place where you are free to speak. As the communication lines become liberated, you can communicate on different levels. Unlock the communication lines and let love in.

## CONVERSATION

There are so many levels of conversation, all of which require a listening ear. A conversation between partners is different to that between children; and a conversation with your parents is different to that with a friend.

Conversation involves us opening up and allowing people into our world. I really believe that we need some guidelines when it comes to conversing with others because of how we perceive what we see and how we think.

My lifelong friend, Nick Sutherland, gave me a book that changed my life. It is called *The Four Agreements: A practical guide to personal freedom* by Don Miguel.

This book taught me the following four lessons, which have helped me navigate the conversations, both good and bad, I've had in my life:

> *Without connection there is no life; it is like a garden with no flowers.*

### 1. Be impeccable with your word

Speak with integrity. Say only what you mean. Avoid using your words to speak against yourself or to gossip about others. Use the power of your word in the direction of truth and love.

### 2. Don't take anything personally

Nothing others do is because of you. What others say and do is a projection of their own reality and dreams. When you are immune to the opinions and actions of others, you won't be the victim of needless suffering.

### 3. Don't make assumptions

Find the courage to ask questions and to express what you really want. Communicate with others as clearly as you can to avoid misunderstandings, sadness and drama. With just this one agreement, you can completely transform your life.

### 4. Always do your best

Your best is going to change from moment to moment; it will be different when you are healthy as opposed to sick. Under any circumstance, simply do your best and you will avoid self-judgment, self-abuse and regret.

These four learnings opened my mind to not be judgmental to others or myself. If you follow these steps, they will free you of taking anything personally and will help you to maintain healthy relationships.

## MY TIPS FOR HOW TO START A CONVERSATION

1. Give someone a compliment and tie it to a question, such as "I love your hair. Do you have a favourite salon that you go to?"
2. Start a general conversation. Here are a few ice breakers: "Have you read any good books lately?" or "What have you been up to since I last saw you?"
3. Ask open-ended questions, such as "Which sports do you enjoy?" "How do you like to spend your weekends?" "What kinds of food do you like to cook?"
4. Ask "if you could only" questions such as "If you could only eat certain foods, what would you like to eat?" "Who would you like to spend the afternoon with?" "If you were stuck on a desert island, who would you like to share it with?"

Your body language is also very important when you are having a conversation. Here are some techniques to improve the positivity of your conversations:

- Always wear a smile
- Open up your posture
- Slightly lean towards the person you're talking to
- Make contact by shaking hands
- Maintain eye contact
- Nod when the other person is talking.

# CONNECTION

*Food is the connector between generations.*

Connection is a key ingredient for our relationships and to create the perfect heart of the table. Research[1] tells us that connecting with each other is not just healthy but it is critical. Our human desire to connect and be part of a larger community is built into our emotional and psychological make-up.

While we see ourselves as individuals with trillions of cells in a body, we are each one cell in a communal body – the universe.

Unfortunately, connecting in our fast-paced modern world is becoming challenging. Spending time with friends and family is becoming more difficult as we are working longer hours. I understand that our lives are busy, however nothing compares to a real heart-to-heart and face-to-face conversation.

Connecting with our elderly family members and bringing up our children sows the seeds of family and responsibility. It is important to listen to our grandparents' stories and incorporate our younger generations in this activity because it creates wisdom in the little ones. It also gives our mentors a sense of dignity where they feel that they are contributing to the family through their own experiences.

Connecting with each other at the table with food creates a trail of seeds for the younger generation to remember as they grow and are challenged with life's obstacles.

Albert Einstein said it so beautifully when he said, "a human being is part of the whole, called by us 'Universe'; a part limited in time and space". Einstein himself experienced his thoughts and feeling as something separated from the rest; a kind of optical delusion of his consciousness. This delusion is a kind of prison for us, restricting us to our personal desires and to affection for only the few people nearest to us. It is our job to free ourselves from this prison by widening our circle of compassion to embrace all living creatures and the whole of nature in its beauty.

When my daughter Josie was younger, I would teach her how to let people into her life. I would tell her that every person is like a home with different rooms. When you meet people, you let them in the front door. However, before you do, you get to know who they are. You don't just let anyone in straight away, do you?

And if you like someone, you invite them into your lounge room and slowly into your kitchen. Then, you create a relationship with them that you are comfortable with, one that frees you to be yourself. You just don't let anyone into your most person room, your bedroom, do you?

Connection is the energy that exists between people. It is what invisibly ties us together and creates a pathway where we feel validated, loved, respected and seen.

# CONVERSING

Different to a conversation, conversing means to take a conversation to another level and truly engage with someone. Nowadays, we are caught up with superficial chitchat and don't care enough about the other person who is sitting across the table to continue the conversation.

Conversing with people opens us up; it's like taking our jacket off and getting ready to talk; it is healthy for our wellbeing and creates a sense of purpose in our lives. Opening up to one another is creating a pathway of communication lines.

## MY TIPS FOR CONVERSING WITH SOMEONE AT THE TABLE

- Listen more than you talk
- Talk about the food and wine
- Ask how their day was and what they've been up to
- Come to an occasion armed with topics
- Tailor the conversation to the listener
- Take your turn in talking and sharing
- Think before you speak
- Don't interrupt someone when they are talking
- Don't talk to only one person when conversing in a group
- Remember, we have two ears and one mouth, which means we should listen twice as much as we speak.

*Food is the connection between the generations; it is the link that binds family together.*

Overall the four principles we've discussed – communication, conversation, connection and conversing – are essential ingredients for healthy relationships. These are the cornerstones of your home and with these you will be able to withstand the challenges that all families have.

These principles will assist you in building your family. The centrepiece of our table is love for our family, and we cover it with the tablecloth of our heritage.

The fifth principle is our tabletop. It is the place where we eat, present our cooking, rest our elbows and place our plates. The tabletop represents the community and without community that is thriving, we will all be isolated. It is the place we all gather together.

We need to feel proud of our community; it is the place we call home, where our children can feel a sense of connection with other people. Where I come from, community is the extension of our home. As the saying goes, it really does takes a village to raise a child.

[1] https://www.psychologytoday.com/us/blog/feeling-it/201208/connect-thrive

# CHAPTER 8 – THE HEART OF THE FAMILY

Picture a healthy heart with all its arteries in place – the blood is pumping and everything is flowing healthily, so it must be a healthy body, right?

The family is the heart of the home. To have a home where everybody is functioning healthily is not a fairy-tale; it is possible. In every family, there is a sequence: we have the matriarch, patriarch and the rest. Each person has a role to perform in order to oversee that everyone is doing okay.

The heart is the most powerful muscle we have. It is crucial to feel, love, live and be loved. We need to constantly activate it until it becomes a pumping force in our lives. We cannot live without our hearts. But how often do we think about how beautiful and strong our heart is? We take it for granted. It's important to remember to think about the heart of our home, to feel the connection to our family.

*The dynasty must thrive not survive.*

## THE MOST BEAUTIFUL HEART: A STORY

One day, in a heavily crowded place there was a young woman who was shouting, "Look at me! I have the most beautiful heart in the world."

Some people stopped and listened to the woman. They saw her heart and were mesmerised by its beauty and they praised her. Then, an old woman approached the young woman and challenged her, saying, "No my daughter, I have the most beautiful heart in the world!"

The young woman responded, "Show me your heart". The old woman revealed her heart; it was old, rough, uneven and had scars all over it. It had lost its shape and appeared to have bits and pieces fused together in different colours.

The young woman started to laugh and said, "Have you gone mad, old woman? See how beautiful my heart is? It is flawless and there is nothing wrong with it! Look at yours, it is ugly. It is full of scars, wounds and blemishes. How can you say you have a beautiful heart?"

The old woman responded, "My dear child, my heart is beautiful. I started my journey with a heart like yours, and I thought my heart was beautiful like you do. Did you see my scars? I am so proud of each one, as each scar represents the love I have shared with a person, the pieces I have given to others and, in return, they have given me a piece of their own heart. This is where I have patched up a piece that was torn away".

The young woman was shocked and speechless as she had never heard any one talk like that before.

The old woman continued, "Since the pieces of my heart I shared were neither equal nor in the same shape or size, my heart is full of uneven edges and bits and pieces. Where my heart has no shape, it is because the pieces of my heart were not loved in return. Your heart looks fresh and full with no scars, which indicates that you never loved or shared love with anybody. Isn't that true?"

The young woman stood still and did not speak a word. Tears rolled down her cheeks and she walked to the old woman and tore a piece of her own heart to give to the old woman.

This lesson taught the young woman that beauty does not come from your outside appearance but rather it comes from within your heart, which is the holder of our own treasure. Our life experiences shape our heart and make it beautiful. Can you relate to this story?

## HEARTFELT EXERCISE: UNLOCKING THE TREASURE WITHIN YOUR HEART

Think about this. We did not have to buy our heart, it was given to us as a gift. It is a treasure that life has given us – a free gift from birth. As long as it beats we are alive. Feel the power of your heart, feel the strength of your heart and how it has guided you to live.

Step into a time in your life when you felt deeply grateful, i.e. after the birth of a child or a family wedding. Breathe in that moment and feel it; the sacredness of that moment, the blessing of that moment. Feel that power internally from your heart.

Think about a moment when you felt your most proud. Shift into that moment, feel that moment, bring that in with the gratitude moment. Think about a sensual romantic moment and bring that into this moment. Think about a time when you laughed out loud and your sides hurt from laughter. Next, bring in a moment that was magical. Now, let's stack all these moments together into your heart and feel that blood pumping with excitement. Feel that heart!

Take this energy into your day and stay focused with loving thoughts in your heart.

*If you found this exercise useful, write down your experiences and what you are grateful for today:*

..................................................................
..................................................................
..................................................................
..................................................................
..................................................................
..................................................................
..................................................................
..................................................................
..................................................................
..................................................................
..................................................................
..................................................................
..................................................................
..................................................................
..................................................................

# CHAPTER 9 – THE WOMEN OF SICILY

***The meaning of life is to find your purpose.***

I want to introduce you to women of calibre, strength, courage, and grace. These are ordinary women who have created extraordinary lives. From their culture and tapestry of heritage, these women of Sicily have created lives of purpose and passion.

In this chapter, these women will share their recipes with you, a little about themselves, their inspiration and how they forged a root from great soil into a new generation.

*Weaving each Sicilian recipe into the future as we remember our past.*

Recipe by recipe, we created a lifetime of memories through food. We are the artists of food from the heart.

For each of the recipes shared in this chapter, personal traits are woven in from the person who taught us how to cook. These special people are remembered each time we create these recipes.

## DR ELIZABETH CELI

*Personal motto: Know thyself. Face Thyself. Be Thyself.*

Dr Elizabeth Celi directs and produces documentaries through the lens of a psychologist and psychic healer. Her documentary 'Remember – our innate connection with planet earth' (currently in production), bridges the gap between the expertise of scientists, metaphysicians, academics and physicians.

These professions all tap into aspects of our bioenergy, spirituality and electromagnetic connection with planet earth. Remembering our innate energy connection with earth reunites us with the alchemy we inherently own.

Elizabeth's 11 years of academic training in psychology, psychophysiology, genetics and clinical depression reflects her integrative health approach over her subsequent 16 years of private practice. Elizabeth's professional speaking, group workshops and private readings open people to quantum level, intuitive energy healing through their exclusive Akashic records.

Elizabeth is intent on reminding people how to pragmatically connect with their intuitive energy and the amazing solutions it holds. Awareness of your intuitive energy is useless if it's not practical. Her Akashic record readings provide each person with over 15 data points which help her clients change parts of their lives that simply aren't working for them anymore.

Making these changes can be confusing or daunting at times. There's a reason for that and our shadow saboteur that meddles with our intellectual and intuitive intelligence knows it very well!

> *Her mother's intellectual tenacity and her father's intuitive strength became pivotal qualities for her, personally and professionally.*

Elizabeth's 12-year journey to completely heal her lower back disc bulge pain through the bioenergy of her intuition is one of several case studies highlighting the shadow saboteur and it's strangle hold on intuitive energy.

Bringing Einstein's energy theories alive, as they relate to our intuition and human consciousness, is a deep passion of Elizabeth's. She is intent on pioneering advances in our *practical* intuition so that our bioenergy resumes its mainstream status again.

**Elizabeth has many strengths, but here are just a few:**

*She is discerning.* Elizabeth has learnt to weigh up both (several) sides of a situation and make informed decisions and judgments. It bugs her when people make judgments without considering more than one side of the story.

*She is resilient.* Setbacks don't set Elizabeth back for long as she re-centres herself quickly and gets on with the next step... and then the next.

*She is intuitive.* Elizabeth truly trusts her gut feelings, which she has learnt to differentiate from her reactive instincts. Elizabeth has built a solid relationship with her intuitive intelligence and consults with it when making decisions for her life and work. This is a comforting foundation for her as she is 'following her feet' while she produces her bioenergy documentary.

*She has a faith.* Elizabeth believe in an all presence – a universal higher consciousness that provides us all, individuals and our societies, with higher order principles to live by. Whatever name people give this – Jesus, Buddha, Divine Mother, Gaia – Elizabeth focuses on the one essence that overlaps in all of them. Her faith rests on spiritual principles that can show themselves in many forms or be explained using different words.

*She wants to be remembered.* Elizabeth wants her legacy to be around helping people to remember and strengthen their connection with their intuitive intelligence and their true gut feelings that powerfully benefit their day-to-day lives. She wants to be remembered as a pioneer in bringing Einstein's energy theories alive as they relate to the human consciousness and intuition.

### ELIZABETH'S TOP THREE CORE BELIEFS:

1. *Integrity matters.* Say what you mean and mean what you say. Integrity builds trust and loyalty.
2. *Say it like it is.* Be honest and courteously straightforward, especially when it's difficult. Holding on to half-truths, lies or deceiving only creates a rod for your own back.
3. *Actions speak louder than words.* While words can express a lot and share profound truth and principle, actions ultimately show what you truly mean and the strength of your integrity. Simple actions are worth more than a thousand words.

---

### A BRIEF DESCRIPTION OF AKASHIC RECORDS ♥

Akashic records are the energy records of who we are. Just as we all have thoughts and feelings on one dimension of energy, the Akashic records are a higher dimension of energy that describe your unique soul level strengths, your soul level memory and all of your choices and consequences creating positive and negative karma. Akashic records are read to rediscover the energetic root cause of any difficulties someone might be having throughout their life. These engrained patterns are transformed by conscious awareness of why the difficulties happen and then use your soul level strengths to fix the problem.

## ELIZABETH'S FAMILY HISTORY

Elizabeth's mother emigrated from the island of Salina, Sicily, to Melbourne, Australia in the early 1960s. She left Elizabeth's two older sisters with her husband (Elizabeth's father) and her mother in Salina. Elizabeth's father was unable to get his initial visa after he lost four of his fingertips in an accident with a World War II grenade. Two years later, Elizabeth's mother was able to bring her family out to Australia.

Elizabeth's father was a labourer alongside her mother, both rebuilding their lives in Australia while Elizabeth and her third sister were born in Melbourne. As the fourth daughter of four (she had no brothers to tease her), Elizabeth recognised that her parents and sisters had many significant life events that created a history of their own before she was born. Their hardships and intense work ethic paved the way for an easier lifestyle by the time she was born.

It was the dream of Elizabeth's parents to give their children a better education than was possible on the islands of Sicily. And this was always in the back of Elizabeth's mind as she pursued her PhD.

Elizabeth's academic training towards becoming a registered psychologist, and the strain it created in helping her realise the importance of her intuitive gut feelings, is something she now speaks about professionally.

Elizabeth's parents' hardships continue to inspire her professional speaking and workshops where she teaches people how to have their intellectual and intuitive energy work together more harmoniously.

## ELIZABETH'S MAMMA'S RECIPE FOR POTATO BROTH SOUP

### Ingredients

1 brown onion

5-10 (depending on size) chopped Roma tomatoes (with the skin left on)

2 whole cloves of garlic

1 tsp. of cinnamon or cinnamon sugar

3-5 small, diced potatoes

Salt and pepper to season

Optional: You may like to add more tomato paste and/or peas to add with the potato

### Method

1. Fry the onion until translucent.
2. Add the chopped Roma tomatoes to the onion.
3. Then, add the garlic cloves.
4. Then, add the cinnamon, and salt and pepper to season.
5. Fry the tomato base for 5 minutes.
6. Add the diced potatoes into the tomato base to infuse.
7. Cook for another 5 minutes.
8. Fill the pot with water until it 'grows' the tomato base to 3/4 the height of the pot.
9. Bring this broth to the boil.
10. If you desire, you could add tomato paste to darken the broth and/or add peas to make a potato and pea broth.
11. When the broth comes to the boil, add pasta and serve with hot crusty bread.

www.drceli.com

THE HEART OF THE TABLE 39

www.facebook.com/RosettaPavone

# ROSETTA PAVONE

*Personal motto: Never say never and don't give up on your dreams.*

Rosetta and Carmela have known each other for several years. Rosetta always says it was inevitable that their paths would merge together at some point.

Carmela and Rosetta share very similar life experiences and stories – they are both women of Sicily (in spirit) and they share the same passion for their Sicilian culture and heritage, which they have both drawn inspiration from to inform their creative and personal aspirations.

Rosetta was three years old when her parents migrated from Sicily to Melbourne, Australia in 1957. As a young girl growing up in the '60s and '70s, she was a square peg in a round hole, culturally dislocated and isolated from the norm. Rosetta learnt from a very young age that she was going to have to fight really hard to find her place in the world and to fulfil her hopes and dreams for her future.

**Rosetta has many strengths, but here are just a few:**

*She is resilient.* Rosetta thanks her Sicilian DNA for her characteristics of determination, resilience, hard work and courage. Confronting her battles head on proved to be rewarding. Sixty years later, Rosetta can now reflect with pride and gratitude for the blessed life that she enjoys with her family today.

*She holds a bachelor's degree.* After working on her career and in her business for over 30 years, Rosetta's children had grown up and graduated from university and it was the right time for her to pursue her long-standing ambitions.

In 2006, Rosetta graduated from Melbourne University with a Bachelor of Fine Arts. As a mature-aged student, her six years of full-time tertiary studies tested all of her abilities.

*She has a faith.* Rosetta's Christian faith has been her guiding strength throughout her whole life.

*She is inspired by Sicilian women.* Through her work as an artist, Rosetta has been able to express her deepest emotions, and the complexities of her Sicilian culture has been the catalyst that has informed her work. In her artwork, Rosetta focuses on female identity and the portrayal of *la donna* as a key figure of family life.

She is always inspired by the resilience of women, their creative talents, the *hand made*, their strength to overcome social and cultural dislocation. Rosetta's last solo exhibition in 2014 was titled 'Donne di Sicilia: Stitch-by-Stitch' and it was a culmination of her years of research expressed in paintings, installations, video, photography and sacred icon paintings. This exhibition was the highlight of her life – she felt honoured and privileged to pay tribute to the many women that continue to inspire her today.

*She wants to be remembered.* Rosetta married her true love and soul mate, Tanino, 43 years ago and they are blessed with two children and four grandchildren. Rosetta wants to be remembered as having inspired her children and grandchildren to be proud of their heritage and she hopes they continue to live out their dreams with love and gratitude.

# ROSETTA'S MOTHER'S RECIPE FOR AMARETTI

## Ingredients

1 cup of icing sugar

4 large egg whites

500g almond meal

1 ¾ cup of caster sugar

2 teaspoons of baking powder

¼ teaspoon of almond essence

multicoloured glazed cherries, halved for decoration

## Method

1. Preheat oven to 170°C and line two baking trays with baking paper.
2. Place icing sugar in a bowl before adding the egg whites and whisk this mixture until it's foamy.
3. In a separate bowl, combine the almond meal, caster sugar and baking powder.
4. Make a well in the centre of the dry mixture and add the almond essence.
5. Gradually add the egg white mixture to the dry ingredients, mixing constantly in a circular motion.
6. Mix thoroughly with your hand to form a sticky dough.
7. Roll a teaspoon of dough into a ball. Roll in icing sugar and place on baking tray. Repeat with remaining mixture.
8. Place a halved cherry in the centre of each biscuit.
9. Bake for 12 to 15 mins or until the biscuits are risen, slightly cracked and very lightly coloured.
10. Cool for 5 minutes before transferring to a wire cooling rack.
11. Enjoy with un buon café!

## FABRIZIA LANZA

*Personal motto: Fabrizia likes to joke about her personal motto as she describes it as 'arm to table'. She misunderstood when people would talk about the farm to table movement, but since she goes out to the garden and picks what will go on her plate, she thinks 'arm to table' is better suited!*

Fabrizia Lanza brings the joys and knowledge of Sicilian food and culture into people's lives around the world. Born in Palermo in 1961, Fabrizia grew up among her family's 200-year-old agricultural estate in the heart of Sicily.

Being part of the renowned Tasca family of *vignerons* (winemakers) meant Fabrizia was immersed into the world of food and wine from birth.

In addition to wine, the estate produces cheese, fresh pasta, poultry, lamb, extra-virgin olive oil and an enormous variety of fruit and vegetables, naturally instilling Fabrizia with the sensory satisfactions of farm to table. Understanding the practices and challenges would come later.

At the age of 18, Fabrizia flew north, spending time in France and Italy to experience other worlds and to study. With a degree in art history, she worked for 25 years in museums and as an art curator, ultimately directing two museums in Feltre, 100 kilometres north of Venice.

Meanwhile, Fabrizia's mother, Anna Tasca Lanza, established the world-renowned Anna Tasca Lanza Cooking School in 1989 to promote Sicilian cuisine; believing that eating well is crucial to the quality of our lives and knowing how to eat well requires an intimate understanding of the land's produce, food preparation methods and the rituals of eating.

In 2006, at the age of 45, Fabrizia decided to join Anna's venture and return to Sicily. Not only would she be closer to her family and reconnect with Sicilian food and its environment, but also her skills and creativity would flourish. In 2010, after the passing of her mother, Fabrizia became director of the school and continues to build on Anna's magnificent legacy.

Continuing in her mother's footsteps, Fabrizia travels regularly to the US to promote Sicilian food, joining good food advocates along the way, including Alice Waters in California and Mario Batali in New York. Fabrizia has written numerous books on Sicilian cuisine, including *The Heart of Sicily, The Flavours of Sicily, Olive: A Global History* and *Coming Home to Sicily* (co-authored with former *Gourmet* magazine editor Kate Winslow).

Fabrizia also promotes Sicilian food practices and traditions through video documentation. Fabrizia produced the documentary 'Amuri: The Sacred Flavors of Sicily' in 2014 alongside Giacomo Costa, Lena Connor and Chiara Pelizzoni and it focuses on the techniques of foods that are in danger of extinction.

In September 2017, Fabrizia launched a Kickstarter campaign to fundraise for her next film 'Amaro', which brings to life the narrative of Sicilian food and culture through the exploration of a single taste: bitterness.

Under Fabrizia's direction, the cooking school's teaching program has been extended, including 'Cook the Farm' – a program where the truly food passionate spend ten weeks at the school exploring food from every angle.

Entering its third year, this program attracts international students who are passionate about bridging the gaps between eating, cooking and farming and who seek to understand food from global, Mediterranean and Sicilian perspectives.

### Fabrizia has many strengths, but here are just a few:

*She is passionate.* Fabrizia is very passionate about what she is doing and she is a very curious person. She loves to learn and everything is an eye opener for her.

*She believes in love.* Fabrizia believes that passion and love can move mountains. She says that if you really want to do something, you can do it – *volere è potere* is what they say in Italian and people recognise when it is good stuff, even in Sicily where the walls of mistrust are unbelievably high.

*Her family is her faith.* Fabrizia's family has and continues to play a huge role in her life, just as in many Italians' lives. Italy is still pretty much a family-based country; lots of children still live with their parents until they are 30+ years old. This is due to unemployment, of course, but also because mothers and families love to keep their 'children' close to home. This can have some negative side effects. And Fabrizia left Sicily when she was 18 years old to escape her family strength and power. She belongs to a large, old Sicilian family and she wanted to move away to prove that she was someone unique and capable of building a life of her own. When she came back, her family was still there, loving and surrounding her with affection. She loved it, and still does today.

*She wants to be remembered.* Fabrizia ran away from Sicily because her family's legacy was too much and she felt she could not express her own voice. But her family's legacy was and is still there and somebody must take care of it. Fabrizia works in the country estate, which has been in her family for the past two centuries and wants to do her part to continue that legacy.

## FABRIZIA'S NONNA'S RECIPE FOR GHINEFFI

This recipe makes approximately 40 to 50 small ghineffi.

### Ingredients

*For the risotto:*
30ml (2 tbsp.) of olive oil
200 grams (8 oz.) of Arborio rice
1 litre (4 cups) of chicken stock, heated
50 grams (½ cup) of grated parmesan cheese
30 grams (2 tbsp.) of butter

*For the batter:*
2 eggs
100 grams (¾ cup) of plain flour
250 ml (1 cup) of water
A bowl of breadcrumbs
Oil for frying (vegetable or olive)

### Method:

1. In a medium saucepan, place the oil and Arborio rice over a medium heat. Toast the rice for a minute or two, or until a slight change in colour occurs.
2. Take the heat to medium-high, then add 1 cup of the heated stock.
3. Allow the stock to boil but stir constantly.
4. When the rice has soaked up the stock, add another cup and boil again while stirring.
5. Once the rice has soaked up this second cup of stock, add another half a cup of stock.
6. When the rice is plump and cooked, take the pot off the heat and add the cheese first, then the butter.
7. On a clean counter or on a baking sheet, spread the risotto, which should be fairly stiff, out into a 1 cm thickness.
8. Allow to cool.
9. Prepare the batter by beating the eggs, then adding the flour and water.
10. Fill a bowl with breadcrumbs.
11. Once the risotto is cooled, roll up into small balls that are approximately 1 cm round.
12. Dip each risotto ball firstly into the batter, then into breadcrumbs and set aside.
13. Once all the balls are rolled and battered, lightly fry in heated frying oil and let them drain on a paper towel.

www.annatascalanza.com/fabrizia-lanza/

# ROSE FARFALLA

*Personal motto: There is really only LOVE. Imagine if that's what we all lived by – LOVE.*

Rose grew up in a typical Sicilian-Italian family – they migrated to Australia and then never changed. Rose was a little Aussie-Italian girl that started kindergarten without knowing a word of English. In primary school, she brought prosciutto and sundried tomatoes for lunch, not a vegemite sandwich! In high school, she wasn't allowed to hang out at the shops after school.

Once she finished school, Rose was the first in her family to open a chain of successful computer retail stores, the first to get a university degree, the first to marry a non-Italian and she was even the first to get divorced. Although her marriage was extremely difficult, Rose was blessed with her little angel Josephine who has given Rose the strength and energy to be the best version of herself.

Fast-forward 12 years and Rose is now married to her soul mate Pat, actually Pasquale Farfalla. With this connection, Rose gained another beautiful daughter, Pat's daughter Annabel, and then their son Noah arrived. Rose is hoping that they are further blessed with another munchkin one day soon. These days, Rose and her family live on the beautiful Mornington Peninsula where she is a stay-at-home mum. She also runs a counselling practice where she help clients reach their full potential and empower them to believe in themselves again.

*Rose has many strengths, but here are just a few:*

*She uses her past to help others.* Rose uses her life experiences to empower and help others see that they too have the power to change their lives and truly live the life they want.

*She has a faith.* Rose believes that her Catholic faith supports and leads her through life. Rose was a divorced single mother at the young age of 25 and after a difficult marriage, she was finally set free from her violent husband on Christmas of 2005.

Rose always longed for her own family and met her soul mate – a man she would be proud to call her husband. It took ten years for her dreams to come true. When she met Pat they had an instant family. They named their son Noah because they felt that he brought them together.

*She is strong.* Rose believes that we are only given the crosses that we can carry. With each challenge in life, we are made stronger and wiser.

*She wants to leave a legacy.* Rose would love to be remembered as a supportive, loving and nourishing mother, a caring wife, daughter, sister, aunty and godmother to Scarlett Zavona.

*She believes that truth is the only answer.* Rose is passionate about people living their best lives. She believes that every single one of us has the power to create the life we truly wish to live and experience.

## ROSE'S MUM'S RECIPE FOR CALAMARI RIPIENI – ELEONORA ZAVONA

### Ingredients

*Calamari*

3 cleaned large squid (calamari)

2 tbs of olive oil

1 clove of garlic, finely chopped

½ cup plain bread crumbs

2 tbs chopped fresh flat-leaf parsley

2 tbs chopped Gaeta olives or other mild black olives

2 tbss chopped, rinsed, and drained capers

½ tsp dried oregano, crumbled

salt and freshly ground black pepper

*Sauce*

¼ cup olive oil

½ cup dry red wine

2 cups chopped canned peeled tomatoes with their juice

1 clove large garlic, lightly crushed

pinch of crushed red pepper

salt

### Method:

1. Make a small slit at the pointed end of each calamari. Rinse thoroughly, letting the water run through the body sac. Drain and pat dry. Separate the bodies from the tentacles with a knife. Set the bodies aside. Chop the tentacles with a large knife or in a food processor.

2. Pour the olive oil into a medium pan. Add the garlic. Cook over medium heat until the garlic begins to turn golden – for approximately one minute. Stir in the tentacles. Cook by stirring for two minutes. Add the bread crumbs, parsley, olives, capers and oregano. Add salt and pepper to taste. Remove from the heat and let cool.

3. With a small spoon, stuff the bread crumb mixture loosely into the calamari bodies, filling them only halfway. Secure the calamari with wooden toothpicks.

4. Choose a pan large enough to hold all of the calamari in a single layer. Pour in the ¼ cup olive oil and heat over medium heat. Add the calamari and cook, turning them with tongs, until they are just opaque, about two minutes per side.

5. Add the wine and bring to a simmer. Stir in the tomatoes, garlic, crushed red pepper and salt to taste. Bring to a simmer. Partially cover the pan and cook, turning the calamari occasionally, until they are very tender (approximately for 50 to 60 minutes). Add a little water if the sauce becomes too thick. Serve hot.

www.rosefarfalla.com

## ENZA CENTORAME

*Personal motto: Chi dorme non prende pesci (the early bird catches the worm)*

At 20 years old, Enza Insabella was married and, since then, has been known as Enza Centorame. Enza was born in 1945 in a little medieval town named Aidone, Sicily. She was the youngest of five children and her family experienced hard times after the war. It was difficult for her parents to raise a family with very little, but Enza's parents managed to keep their children feeling loved and happy.

Enza remembers that her parents were very creative when it came to cooking family meals. They only had few ingredients, but they always managed to make enough good food. This is how Enza learned to create an 'adventure' in the kitchen with whatever they managed to get on that particular day. This experience was enriching for Enza as, even to this day, she can create a meal from very little and even though she can go to the supermarket and buy anything she wants, she still gets a buzz when someone gifts her produce.

### Enza has many strengths, but here are just a few:

*She has a deep love for 'her' Sicily.* This love inspired Enza to start her business Savouring Sicily, which has given her the opportunity to introduce many people to the history, beauty and culture as well as the delicious food that has developed from centuries of past occupation by a diverse and ancient variety of cultures.

*She has a faith.* Enza believes in God and the universe. She believes that the more you think of other people and help those around you, it allows for many doors to open and a wealth of blessings to meet you.

*She believes in communication.* To Enza, communication is number one. She believes that there aren't many problems that cannot be solved by sitting around the table with a loving heart and good intentions! With communication comes connectivity. Enza has always delighted in meeting new people and she has gained valuable strength from these friendships and connections.

*She is writing a book.* Enza hopes that by writing her book, *The Ingredients of Influence*, she will leave good memories for her grandchildren, Thomas (who is now a chef) and Frank. Enza spends a lot of time with Thomas and Frank 'playing' with the freshest ingredients from her garden and creating Sicilian meals while answering all the questions that children have about 'the olden days'.

## ENZA'S FAMILY'S RECIPE FOR CONDIMENTS

## PESTO AL FINOCCHIETTO SELVATICO (PESTO WITH WILD FENNEL)

Wild fennel is often found growing in your garden or in open countryside, especially by riverbanks. Next time you're on a country walk – keep an eye out for some fennel to use in this recipe!

### Ingredients

A generous bunch of tender fennel tips (approximately 200 grams), washed and dried

100 grams pine nuts

200 ml olive oil

1 large garlic clove

1 tsp salt

1 tsp chilli flakes

100 grams grated pecorino cheese

Optional: you could also add anchovies

### Method

1. Put all the ingredients except for the cheese, in a blender and blend until creamy.
2. Remove from blender and fold in the cheese.
3. This condiment will last for up to two weeks in the fridge.

## CIPOLLATA ALL'AGRODOLCE (SWEET AND SOUR ONIONS)

### Ingredients

6 onions

200 ml olive oil

100 ml balsamic vinegar

2 tbs sugar

1 tsp salt

### Method

1. Peel and slice the onions into halves, making sure to slice them instead of chop.
2. Cook the onions in the olive oil and salt for about 10 minutes until they look soft, transparent and not too fried.
3. Add vinegar and cook for five more minutes.
4. Add the sugar before increasing the temperature and stir often – cook only for two minutes and it's ready!
5. This condiment will last for at least two weeks in the fridge.

www.savouringsicily.com

## CARMELA AMATO D'AMORE

*Personal motto: I cannot change the circumstances of my life, but I can change my attitude.*

As I am the author of this book, you'll know a lot about my family history, Sicilian background and passions by now. However, as a proud Sicilian woman, I wanted to share more with you here, among my fellow women of Sicily.

I am the daughter and granddaughter of Sicilian immigrants – cooks of the past, fishermen and fisherwomen who brought their trades with them when they moved to Australia. I am proud of my heritage; it is the foundation that I have built my life on. I am a daughter, wife, mother, nonna and a mentor to many. I have come full circle as I found my identity in *cucina povera* and love cooking from centuries-old recipes; perfecting them and adding my own flair.

### MY STRENGTHS

*I am courageous.* Courage has been with me since I can remember. It took courage for me to wake up, approach the obstacles that were before me. My culture has shaped, refined and forged me.

*I have a strong sense of duty.* Ever since I was a young girl, I felt a sense of duty to do the right thing and to be my best self towards other people. I used to find it very difficult to speak to other people. However, I have learned to overcome this when, as the eldest daughter, I had to step up and be the spokesperson for my parents as they could not speak English.

A sense of duty does not have to be restricting – when it is used to generate freedom, duty can liberate many. I feel a sense of duty to act as a link between the generations of my family – it is my responsibility to pave a healthy pathway for my children and their children. I respect my ancestors, but it's time to do things differently. The times are changing and so must we, lest we become redundant.

I am a voice for the future generations, setting the tone for them and helping them to find value in their pasts to enhance their future and, in doing so, enhancing my own.

*I have a faith.* My faith is in the unseen as I can believe in things that have yet to take place. I can create, through vision, purpose and belief, a greater power outside of myself.

I believe in God, the father of all creation, in Jesus his son and the Holy Spirit who is my guide and teacher. I also believe that the universe is my playground. I believe in the angels that are in my life, and I believe that one person can change the lives of many.

*Life is a journey – one that I will never properly finish, but I will have fun and enjoy it as I go along.*

*I believe in myself.* The power of my thoughts are what shape my life; changing the way I look at things has changed the way I think, feel, love and give. Believing in myself has been a journey into a new world of creating my own beliefs.

*I want to leave a legacy.* My legacy is my children and grandchildren; they are the traits of my ancestors and every one of them is unique and wonderfully made. I will leave this world in a better place by leaving them in it. I also want to leave a legacy from educating people about Sicilian cooking. It is my passion, which flows from the experiences of my life, and to teach my students how to cook beautiful Sicilian food is the best way that I can make a lasting impact, long after I'm gone.

The recipe I am sharing with you on the following pages is very dear to my heart. It was originally my Nonna Carmela's recipe, which my Mother Sarina updated. I have since updated the recipe and when I cook it, I remember the steps from observing both the women who influenced my life.

# MY FAMILY RECIPE FOR POLPETTI DA NONNA

## POLPETTI DI PESCE DA NONNA (NONNA'S FISHBALLS)

### Secret key ingredients

Take time to make this meal and turn your phone off!

Put a nice, relaxing Italian song in the background. I recommend 'E Ritorno Da Te' by Laura Pausini

Enjoy a glass of Grillo from Sicily, my favourite!

### Ingredients

1 kg of diced fresh fish i.e. sardines, garfish or whiting

1½ cups of grated pecorino – no pepper

1½ cups of old bread soaked in milk and then drained

½ cup of diced fresh parsley

4 eggs, whisked and beaten with added sea salt and cracked pepper

1 clove of garlic, crushed

A small bowl of warm water

Olive oil for frying

### Method

1. Place all of the ingredients in a large mixing bowl and use your hands or a wooden spoon to mix well, but gently.

2. Wet your hands with the warm water and start to make the polpetti (meatballs). I like them to be around the size of my palm and I flatten them to be approximately 2 inches wide.

3. Line a baking tray with greaseproof paper and place each polpetta on the tray, always dipping your hands in the warm water before picking up the next.

4. When you have finished, heat the olive oil in a frying pan on medium heat. Once the oil is hot enough, place the polpetti in the pan.

5. I like to use a fork and a tablespoon when I cook the polpetti, turning each polpetta with the same technique my mother used – with the fork in my left hand and the spoon in my right, I turn them over slowly. Remember to turn them slowly and gently as fish is delicate and needs your assistance to keep it together.

6. Once the polpetti are cooked, place them on a tray with a fresh sheet of greaseproof paper. This will soak up any access oil and is healthier.

You can either top your polpetti with my aioli dressing (see the next recipe) or cook them in my Napoli sauce recipe from *Carmela's Cucina Povera* for another 20 minutes and add your favourite pasta. Remember, when you place your polpetti in the sauce (for about 10 minutes), add fresh basil and garlic as this will lift up the flavours and taste amazing!

## CARMELA'S RECIPE FOR A QUICK AIOLI SAUCE

### Ingredients

250 grams of gluten-free mayonnaise

1 tbs of fresh, crushed garlic

1 lemon, freshly squeezed juice

½ tablespoon of fresh dill

Cracked pepper

### Method

1. Place all the ingredients into a food processor and mix for two minutes.
2. If you don't have a food processor, don't worry! You can put the ingredients in a mixing bowl and whisk it all together.
3. *Note:* you can make your own mayonnaise with egg yolks, Dijon mustard, olive oil, garlic and a little lemon juice.

You will notice that Sicilian food has a lot of polpetti and involtini in its recipes. This is because our nonnas cooked from a place of love, using their two hands, with their family in the middle of their hearts. When you make these recipes, I would love for you think of your loved ones and how much you love them, creating healing by cooking from the heart.

Just as I have shared stories of my women of Sicily. I would love for you to take some time to think about your own story. Use this space to start your journey:

### What are your strengths?

..............................................................................

..............................................................................

..............................................................................

..............................................................................

..............................................................................

..............................................................................

### What do you believe in?

..............................................................................

..............................................................................

..............................................................................

..............................................................................

..............................................................................

..............................................................................

### What is your personal motto?

..............................................................................

..............................................................................

..............................................................................

..............................................................................

..............................................................................

..............................................................................

### What do you want your legacy to be?

..............................................................................

..............................................................................

..............................................................................

..............................................................................

..............................................................................

..............................................................................

..............................................................................

..............................................................................

### What do you want for your family? ♥

..............................................................................

..............................................................................

..............................................................................

..............................................................................

..............................................................................

..............................................................................

..............................................................................

..............................................................................

# CHAPTER 10 – WHY I LOVE SICILIAN FOOD

*Sicilian food is God's kitchen shared across the table.*

And God created Sicily, the place where the mountains meet the sea. Sicily, the island in the sun, is home to heavenly beaches. It's the Italy you never knew existed. It is a place where time and tradition have been constructed by the people and their faith.

The culture is like no other place in the world – its influence is noticeable from the delicious delicacies of our food. Historically, Sicilian cuisine has been influenced by many different cultures, Byzantines, Greek, Spanish, French, Norman, Albanian, Jews, Romans, Arabs, and this makes it complex, interesting and full of passion.

The fragrance spices we use are especially evident in the markets of Palermo and Catania. Follow your nose and you will find them or they will find you.

## A LITTLE STORY ABOUT SICILY

I want to share with you the legend of where the name *Trinacria* comes from.

As the story goes, there were once three nymphs who danced around the world, taking handfuls of the earth, small stones and different fruits from the most beautiful and fertile places.

They stopped in a region of the universe that had a particularly clear blue sky. There, the dance became more elegant, joyful and between one step and another the three nymphs threw into the sea everything they had collected from the world. The sea lit up like a rainbow and from the waves emerged a whole new rich, fragrant and gleaming land.

It was shaped like a triangle as it filled the space between the headlands that had been created right there where the dancing nymphs had thrown everything they had found.

Today, we call this place Sicily.

## WHY IS SICILIAN FOOD SO EXCITING?

Sicilian food is seasonal and healthy; we work the land and fish the produce, so you are eating the food of God's land. That is why it is known today as God's kitchen.

For nearly 2,000 years, the gastronomic culture of Sicilian cibo has been influenced by all the people who have passed through. The food culture has been handed down from one generation to the next, becoming a sign of identity for all Sicilians both in Sicily and around the world.

There is a sweet flavouring symphony in your palate. Its spices and aromatic plants, such as basil, oregano, mint, rosemary and sage form the seasoning base of all Sicilian recipes.

## WHY DO I WANT TO TALK TO YOU ABOUT SICILIAN FOOD?

I am passionate about Sicilian food as it is the foundation of my life. The love for Sicilian food is built from a nonna's sacrifice and her love for her family. It is based on the Virgin Mary's love for Jesus and on the community that extends into the nation. Even if you are not a believer, the method works as it comes from the purity of loving others.

A nonna's role is one of a mentor and martyr as she sacrifices all of her life to build a family. We must recognise that this takes hard work, don't you agree? A nonna is the beacon in the night – she is the navigator of the family, she directs, leads and calls. Her voice is the gospel of God.

Today, we can learn from our nonna and use her as a role model for the future. However, think young women of today shouldn't try to be martyrs like their elders have been – we have entered a new age.

Love is the force that will navigate us through this course. We must listen to our children and grandchildren, direct them when we can see their potential for the future and allow them to make their own decisions. By making their own decisions, our future generations will gather experiences and create their own lives full of purpose and passion. Where once we were there to dictate, today we are there to guide.

The same can be said about Sicilian food. It is unique (just like our children) and all the recipes are masterpieces that are woven into our culture, families and communities.

> *Sicilian food is made of changing shapes, vibrant colours, intense flavours and fragrances – green and red blend together, sweet and savoury embrace, it has its own melody and symphony like no other culture.*

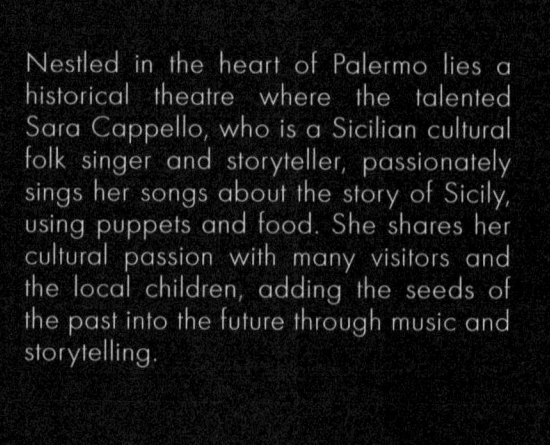

Nestled in the heart of Palermo lies a historical theatre where the talented Sara Cappello, who is a Sicilian cultural folk singer and storyteller, passionately sings her songs about the story of Sicily, using puppets and food. She shares her cultural passion with many visitors and the local children, adding the seeds of the past into the future through music and storytelling.

## SHARING A LITTLE FROM GOD'S KITCHEN

### Bread – il pane

I do not apologise for my biased opinion here as I have tasted food across the world, and there is no other taste that satisfies my palate like Sicilian food. In Sicily, bread is baked twice a day in the local villages. The flour is made with the flavour of *il panetiere* (the baker) and their passion. In countryside farms, the bread is still made in wood-fired ovens using flour that is durum semolina (from the grain semola), which is golden yellow in colour and a finer grind of semolina than that used to make dried pasta. The finer grind is known in Sicily as *farina di semola rimacinata*.

Sicilian bakers are proud of their heritage and work with passion to continue the legacy. They are a special breed of artisanal individuals who create art for you to share across the table, to enjoy the flavour and the time that it took to create the perfect loaf of bread.

### Pasta – la pasta

Semolina durum wheat is a specialty, but the last time I visited Sicily I discovered tumminia, an ancient grain that is low-GI and contains less gluten. It is so tasty! It is mixed with wholegrain to create a fusion of taste across the palate in pasta and bread.

I love making pasta with my friend and partner from Go-Sicily, Annalisa Pompeo. When I take guests on tours of Sicily, I make sure to spend many delicious days with her while she teaches my guests and I about the region of Agrigento and we enjoy the countryside and travel around this magnificent part of Sicily – not a place to miss if you are in this part of the world!

To find out more about Go-Sicily, visit www.go-sicily.it

*To create a dish with the perfect ingredients, make a plate of pasta with seasonal produce and enjoy at the table.*

### Tomatoes and eggplants – pomodori e melanzane

Tomatoes arrived in Sicily thanks to the Spanish and eggplants arrived from the native land of southern India, probably from the Romans on the eastern fringes of their empire.

There is an enormous list of Sicilian recipes that are created using these two ingredients. Today, we have Tunisian eggplants that come from the tip of Africa and they are light purple, huge and full of flavour. Eggplants originally came to Sicily from India and Sri Lanka – just a few of the many influences of trading in Sicily.

These two ingredients have created dishes upon dishes that are enjoyed in homes, restaurants and shared across the table with a glass of wine and laughter.

THE HEART OF THE TABLE  53

### Fish and meat – *carne e pesce*

Seafood is the preferred meat in Sicily – we fry, bake and chargrill our seafood. The traditional meat in Sicilian cuisine is goat and lamb.

These meats are part of the history of Sicily and Italy; they have been, and continue to be, consumed with various dishes. These ingredients continue the traditional table, but allow for a modern twist.

I have spent many hours at the fish market in Isola Delle Femine with my friend Mario Puccio who is a magnificent Sicilian chef from the town of Capaci in Palermo. He is so talented and he teaches his students about Italian food at his restaurant, Puccio, which his family have owned for nearly 40 years!

For more information about Mario Puccio and Ristorante Puccio, visit www.ristorantepuccio.it

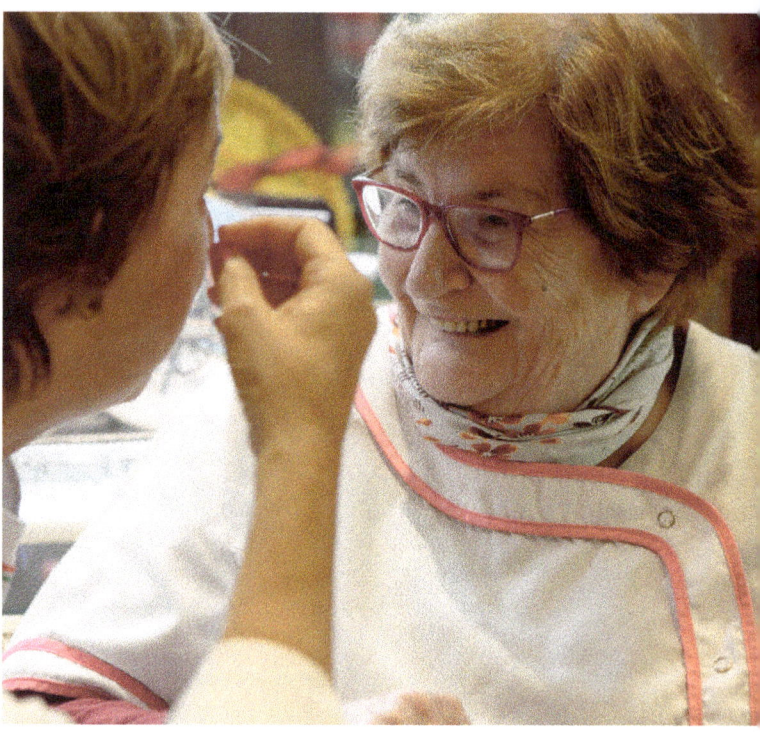

### Cheeses – *formaggi*

Caciocavallo, fiore di late, pecorino, e latte ovino, ricotta, bocconcini and parmigiano are cheeses that are the icons of Sicily. Think of the wonderful Sicilian families who have been artisan cheese makers for generations – we owe them a great deal! It truly is a reverence as they have shared their knowledge with us so that we can grate tasty formaggi on our favourite dishes or enjoy with a crusty loaf of bread and a glass of wine at our table.

Every year on my annual culinary tour I visit my friend Giacinto Cangelosi who has a beautiful place up in the Madonie mountains in the heart of Sicily. He is a fifth-generation shepherd and together we make cacciocavallo cheese and ricotta cheese. It is beautiful to spend the whole day breathing the mountain air and enjoying this rustic atmosphere in Piano Farina.

> Maria Grammatico is the queen of Sicilian pasticceria. She resides in the mountain of Erice, which is a Norman village with little shops and cobble-stone roads and this is where she has her cooking school where she mentors others and shares her expertise. Maria is inspirational, she has so many talents and skills as a pastry chef and her sweets are very enticing! You can learn more about Maria from her book, *Bitter Almonds*, which is a story of hard times, courage and grace, or by visiting her website www.mariagrammatico.it

### Sweets – il dolci e la fruitta

The cassata was influenced from the Arabs, torrone, mandorla, frutti di pasta reale, gelataria; sorbet comes from the Arab word sharbat. Granita, grapes, figs, prickly pears and watermelon are dried and kept during the months when they are not in season. Once preserved, these ingredients are used to decorate our cakes and desserts.

Gelato is another prominent sweet that we enjoy eating and making in Sicily. How many times have we had a gelato and enjoyed the intense flavours in our mouth? How many times has gelato quenched our thirst? I will always appreciate the time it takes for an artisan pastry chef or nonna to make a delicious cassata. These dishes all represent a heritage, a story, a past to share across our table.

### Street food – mangiare per la strada

In Sicily, you will find long lines of people waiting to be served by the local street food vendor, panni con la milza, arancina, panelle, crochette, melanzane a quaglia.

In Palermo, there is Antonino Buffa nicknamed as Nino u Ballerino. There is a slight dance he does while he is working as he enjoys his passion of food with his patrons. His street food is ranked first in Sicily and fourth in the world! Want to find out more about Nino? Visit his website www.ninouballerina.it

Sfincione is a thick Sicilian pizza topped with tomatoes, onions, a few anchovies, grated cacciocavallo cheese, toasted breadcrumbs and a dash of oregano and it is the oldest style of pizza served by local street vendors. When I visit Sicily every year, I make sure to pick up a sfincione from a young man at the beginning of the Capo mercato (one of the three oldest markets in Palermo). His father taught him how to make the sfincione and he is very proud that he continues the tradition of this historical dish.

One of the best ways to see the markets of Palermo and Catania is to join Marco Romeo from Streaty tours as he takes you to all the main attractions of the town and the markets. On his tour, you will visit Capo, Vucciria and Ballaro and your tastebuds will enjoy many spices and different types of food that you have never tasted before. You also get to enjoy the delicious street food – it is not a tour to miss out on! Find out more information on their website www.streaty.com/#palermo

### The quality – la qualita

In Sicily, our ingredients are flavoursome and have been grown in countryside farms (campagna). We never cook with a product that is out of season because it does not have the same flavour or nutrition for our wellbeing. Every ingredient has its time to develop and its nutritional value.

The markets are full of seasonal produce from the campagnas and the shopping is done every day – eating fresh food is part of the every-day ritual in Sicily and we take it very seriously. My experience has taught me that quality is better than quantity. Value is worthwhile and what we put into our bodies is the result of what we become.

### What do you love about Sicilian food?

..................................................................
..................................................................
..................................................................
..................................................................
..................................................................

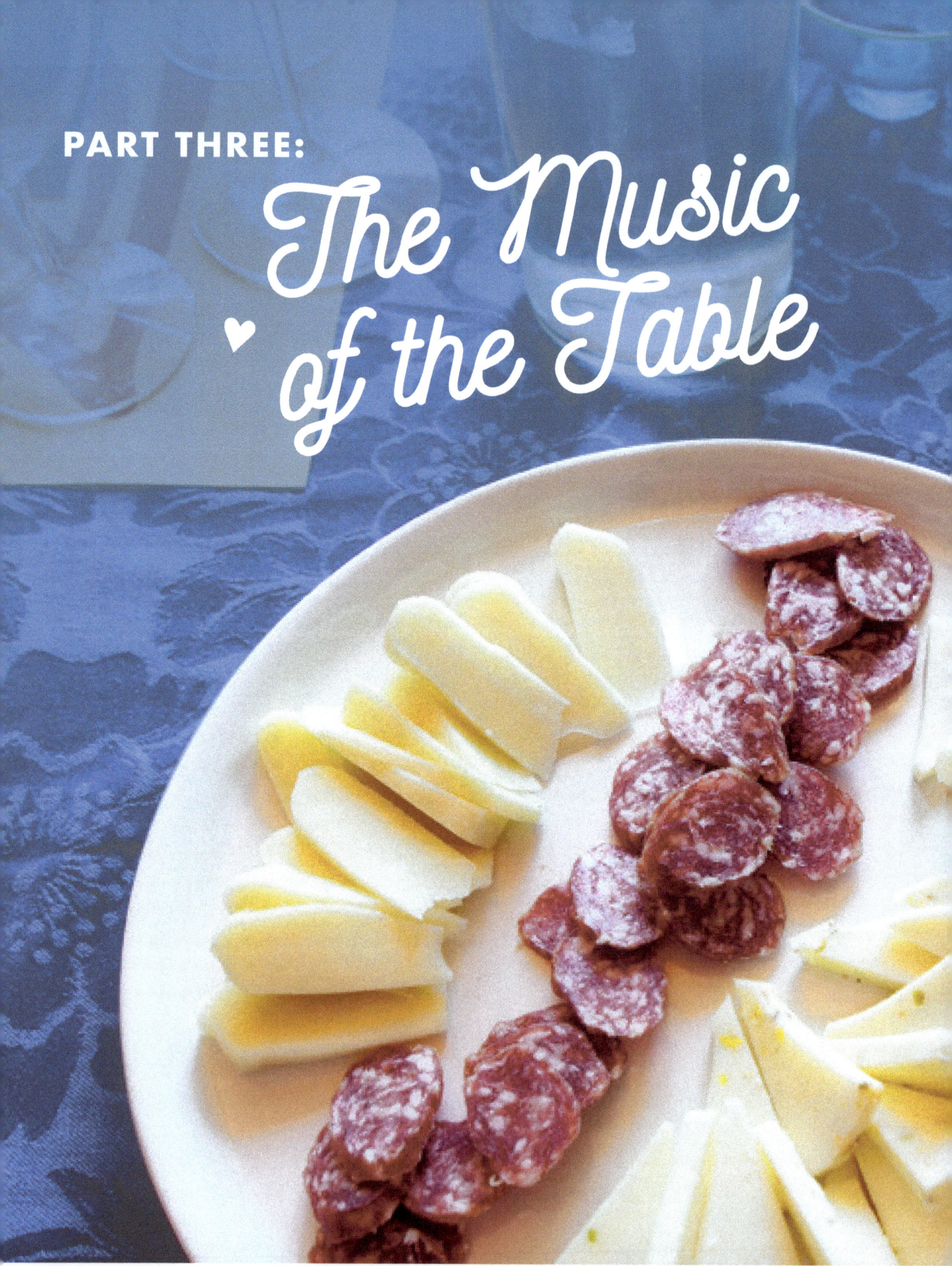

**PART THREE:**

*The Music ♥ of the Table*

# CHAPTER 11 – LET THE MUSIC PLAY ACROSS YOUR TABLE

*La tavola is where the magic begins.*

Research shows that we are starving ourselves because our lives are too busy[2]. We are choosing to order takeout most nights just to feed the family and because we don't have enough time to cook a proper meal. Do we not realise that food is the fuel to our health and wellbeing?

I can hear my nonna say 'Basta! Enough, what are you doing?'

Think about those unique and special times where you sat across the table from your loved ones and ate a meal together. I think you'll agree that in those times, there is a certain melody that brings everyone together, without the need for actual music. We cannot give up on the music that plays across our tables – the laughter and chatter of family gathered together, enjoying moments in life, creating and building memories that will last for generations.

Good food requires patience and time to create, and the recipe also needs to be appreciated. Setting aside time to cook from a recipe and enjoy the ingredients to share across the table is good for the health and wellbeing of our families.

It is up to us to continue the circle of the table for the next generation. It is up to us to stand between the generations, bringing the tradition of family into this new millennium.

There are traditions that need to be awakened – when they are remembered and practised, they become what we see and do every day. Our traditions become mirrored without words through our faith and belief.

It is up to you to set the music of your table in motion. Building a happy family is a work in progress; it takes time, diligence and perseverance.

What do you want your family to remember? What kind of music do you want across your table? Be the hero – create the music of your own family and make it shine. Finding this treasure takes patience but once you have found it, patience and timing will create a symphony and then you will see that it was all worth it.

### THE MUSIC OF ITALY

*Sophia Loren* is an Italian icon, actress and sex symbol with her own unique style and trademark – she manages to incorporate Italian food into her brand as well!

*Luciano Pavarotti* set in motion the music of Italy. His voice was, and still is, the melody that creates sheer pleasure when you hear it. His ravenous appetite for Italian food could never be satisfied!

Both of these wonderful Italian musicians reveal a treasure of their own uniqueness to this world.

[2] Ryan, 2014. 'Busy lifestyles mean that young people might not be learning enough food skills to stay healthy', The Journal.

## OLD RECIPES

Take those old recipes out of the cupboards, ask your mother about the food you remember her cooking as a child. If you are blessed and still have your nonna, ask her to help you to write down her favourite recipes; do it now and then share those recipes with your family and loved ones.

*Create music that will cause a curiosity from strangers, who will want to sit in the symphony with you.*

This is the music of food – the recipes that are from your heritage, the ones that have been passed down from family members, the union of souls from your past, the little DNA that is in you, from them.

Even though it's easy for me to say all this, it does require diligence to cook from an old recipe and it requires time management to eat at proper meal times. However, you will find that your diligence will pay off in time and, when you look back, you will reap the rewards from setting aside time to share a meal with your loved ones. Listen to the music of your heart.

# CHAPTER 12 – THE PERFECT RECIPE

*The perfect ingredients around your table are a pinch of laughter and a splash of love.*

## THE ORIGINS OF THE RICETTA

Have you ever thought about what is in a recipe? Where did it come from? How was it mastered to such perfection? I have often thought about many of these questions, and the thought has nudged me into thinking about the structure of the recipe itself.

Who was the person that put so much thought into creating the recipe? Was it handed down to them from their mother, grandmother, father, grandfather, favourite aunt or uncle or a neighbour?

The definition of 'recipe' is a set of instructions for preparing a particular dish, including a list of the ingredients required. In Italian, it is called *ricetta* which when translated means 'prescription'. I understand this to mean that the maker is required to use the exact, precise ingredients for the recipe and not change or edit anything.

Handing down a recipe to the next generation takes precise timing because it is important that the recipient is given this knowledge when they are ready to receive it as a gift. It is also of upmost importance that the recipient has the competence to continue the tradition. As the receiver of a family recipe, you have some big shoes to fill! You will have to practise until you have perfected the recipe. It might take you your entire life to master, but I guarantee you would do your best to continue the family formula.

*A recipe that is handed down through the generations of a family is a family heirloom – the one who holds it, feels precious and important.*

## THE INGREDIENTS

Now, I would like to take you into the next process: the ingredients. The definition of 'ingredients' is any of the foods or substances that are combined to make a particular dish. They are the glue to the recipe; for without those ingredients, it would be impossible to create the recipe itself. If we changed or altered an ingredient in a family recipe that had been passed down to us from generation to generation, we would miss out on experiencing the full enjoyment and history of the meal.

*The ingredients are the soul of the recipe; you could change them, but the meal would not be the same.*

## THE FLAVOUR

Stick with me. I want to take you into the flavour. Once we know the recipe and the ingredients, it is the flavour that seals the heirloom together. As soon as we put the ingredients together and we taste our recipe, we know exactly how it should taste, we know the emotions that it should bring up and, most of all, the recipe should conjure our memories that are stored in the chronicles of our soul.

## ENHANCING A RECIPE

Although I have already spoken about honouring your family's traditional recipes, there is also a way to incorporate yourself into those recipes, to enhance it, but this requires you to be precise and to master the recipe itself before you try.

The traditional recipe is the framework. As the seasons change, so do the ingredients, and this makes new ideas and inventions possible as we add our own flair to the recipe. I truly believe that each recipe has a life. It is passed down from its first creator to each generation, but as the generations grow and evolve, we can add the ingredients of different lives and experiences to the recipe and it will become a family recipe instead of a recipe from the past.

## CONNECTING WITH THE PAST

These old recipes are time travellers; they transport us like a flash to the exact time and place that we were first introduced to the recipe and the bearer themself comes back to life.

In these moments, we have shifted from the place we're in and what we were doing to acknowledging the universe and sharing a moment in time with our loved one. That is the power of the family heirloom, it is a *tesoro* (jewel or treasure).

For me, a recipe is like life – it takes time to perfect and the more experience we have, the better we become at succeeding. It is up to us to share it with our family, friends and with everyone we come into contact with. Do you have the perfect recipe to share across your table with loved ones?

*Write down a recipe that means a lot to you:*

................................................................
................................................................
................................................................
................................................................
................................................................
................................................................
................................................................
................................................................
................................................................

*Who would you like to share this recipe with?*

................................................................
................................................................
................................................................
................................................................
................................................................
................................................................
................................................................

## THE PERFECT RECIPE

The framework of this recipe
requires heart and soul.

It comes from the foundations;
from the tree of life from heritage and family.
As the scale measures each ingredient
we find that perfect balance.

It is a challenge to create this recipe
as I search for the perfect ingredients.
Each one has been picked with precision;
assisting the search for the equilibrium
in this perfect recipe.

Every ingredient is necessary
for perfection.

When I mould, make
and create
patience and time are gently with me
in the background the seasons teach me.

Permitting this recipe to reach its perfection.
The contrast is there like the indicator
when I put too many ingredients or not enough.

I can taste it.
Each ingredient
has a role to play.
The precision, timing and method are critical.

As I listen gently to the voice of truth
I know which one is right.
I pour these ingredients.
Gently I mix and mould them with perfect precision.

The process of timing requires the unfolding of its work,
patience and alignment.

I get share it with you.
Together we taste the delicious flavour
as it nourishes our wellbeing.
We taste the time and effort it took to make.
With every bite you know the work that went in.

Sharing this recipe with you,
it sparks a light in you
to create your own recipe.

We taste the flavour being the key
when we create the perfect recipe.

We share it with family and friends
the recipe of life becomes alive in you and me.

# CHAPTER 13 – RECIPES FROM THE HEART

**Open your heart to the simple pleasures of life around the table.**

There is nothing that beats the comfort of your home – the security from the hustle of the outside world, closing the doors at the end of the day and feeling content within. Your home is a space where no one can invade, it's where your family resides and settles down from the rest of their days – it's where the heart expands and life stands still.

One of my favourite ways to spend time in my home is to have friends over for dinner. It is a great opportunity to bond with other people and share our experiences and learn from one another. It is also a time to share your favourite recipes with people other than your family, who have most likely not tasted them before.

If you have a special recipe that you're ready to tell a story with, share it across your table. Let your family and friends have a taste; it will create magic. It will become timeless. Your recipes from the heart are treasures to share with each person at the table, while you unlock the past and give your treasured recipes a future.

Food created with love and shared with those who mean the most to you creates memories that last a lifetime.

## THE ITALIAN HEART

Walking you into this heart – the spirit of Italy – is the only way that I can explain to you how wonderful and majestic it is; it is a true treasure cave. It comes from the core of creation, from the universe that has been designed specially to celebrate `the love for life'.

*Home is the place where you just get to be; you can park yourself and stay within the sanctuary of your family and grow together as a family.*

Imagine the green stretching from the Apennine Mountains to the Tyrrhenian Sea, spreading through the landscape and the scent of the Mediterranean ocean. The ruggedness of the Alps and the highest points around Monte Rosa, peaking into Switzerland and along Mont Blanc, touching the peak in France.

The Italian name for heart is *cuore*, meaning depth and strong roots and life is what keeps it alive. Food is what nourishes the heart and keeps it active.

The Italian heart is unique; it is made up of spaghetti, pizza, romance, passion, charisma, volume, fashion, chaos, gestures, music, uniquity, exquisiteness, art, culture and history.

## FOOD IS LIFE

Food is at the very centre of the Italian heart as we love to enjoy the taste and smell of the richest parts of life – food is life for Italians.

Our lust for food is not an excuse to eat, but rather it is a celebration of life. Life is not to be taken for granted. We are here for a reason, to enjoy and celebrate the seasonal produce that still exists today, but we can use this produce to step into our family history using our family recipes passed down from the previous generations. Family is the root from which this heart comes from.

*The heart is the tree of life with the music that food brings across our table.*

## WE LOVE TO CELEBRATE

In the Italian heart, family bonds are very strong and we take this and extend it into the community. We particularly love to share this unity through festivities and events.

Festivities are the joyous part of the Italian heart. Celebrations of all kinds are an excuse to enjoy the company of our family, friends and neighbours. Any opportunity to enjoy and celebrate is a priority in this heart.

We also love to celebrate the small pleasures of life such as enjoying a cup of coffee with friends, going for a stroll with your loved ones, enjoying the smell of the ocean and the mountains and having a picnic.

## OUR HISTORY KEEPS US STRONG

The Italian heart is old and strong like an olive tree, sweet like a prickly pear. Love, passion and grace run through our veins and respect, gallantry and honour are part of our skin. The Italian heart is wild like the sirocco wind and love is what tames it. It is ignited with the fire from the volcanic islands.

Children are the extension of the root and the elderly are honoured for their commitment to building the family, for the next generation are our future.

*Passion for life is what keeps the Italian heart pumping.*

Our elderly family members are given reverence as they have taken the family and nourished it like a delicate plant. Once the plant has taken its shape, the gardener allows it to blossom, tending it every now and again, making sure that it will survive.

## OUR VALUES

The values of the Italian heart have been handed down from previous generations and our values will continue with each heartbeat into the future generations.

Here are some of the values that are important to me and my family:

- Always welcome friends and family and be hospitable
- It is essential to understand the importance of family
- Respect your grandparents (nonna and nonno) and elderly members of the community
- Always eat fresh seasonal produce and have a veggie garden
- Appreciate good quality
- Value dignity and respect
- Enjoy your life
- Have a strong work ethics and an entrepreneurial spirit
- Learn how to overcome obstacles
- Live your life courageously.

The Italian heart is infectious and is all about good food, loving others and celebrating life. I want to share the values of the Italian heart with you to inject infectious love, joy and laughter into your life so that you will be awakened forever in this heart.

I want you to know that you only need to be guided to the entry of the heart. It has always been there, waiting patiently inside you. All you need to do is choose the right time to embrace it and step into a life of love. Welcome.

### What are the values of your heart?

..................................................................
..................................................................
..................................................................
..................................................................
..................................................................
..................................................................

# CHAPTER 14 – TRANSFORM YOUR TABLE INTO MUSIC

*There is a gentle transformation that music brings to the soul of the table.*

If you listen closely, you can hear the music of your table. Sometimes we shut our ears to this and, if this is you, are you ready to rise and create your own music?

Let's look at what the word 'transform' means: to change in form, appearance, structure, metamorphose. It's about the momentum, this is the now.

Think about music and how it soothes you as you listen to it. It creates a melody in your mind and soul, it lingers for hours as you quietly enjoy the sound. Just as music soothes us, food does too as it soothes our palate, our hunger and when you cook in the kitchen, the whole house benefits from a feeling of wellness, don't you think?

The pleasure that food brings to a hungry person is hard to describe with words. Imagine a world without food and music – we would be a lot poorer for it.

## TIPS FOR TRANSFORMING YOUR TABLE

- Set the table properly, asking each family member to help with a certain part of the table setting
- Create a rule where everyone at the table must turn off their digital devices
- Don't answer the phone at meal times; you can always call back later
- Create a positive environment where everyone can enjoy each other's company
- Open up the communication lines by telling stories
- Plan your evening meals for the week by asking each family member to put forward their choice of meal
- Create unity through good food
- Invite your children into the kitchen when you are cooking to keep you company or to just observe. This way cooking becomes a family activity, not a cooking lesson. They will soon dive in when they feel ready.
- Focus on enjoying the moment rather than making the perfect meal. Stay positive when things don't turn out perfectly – life is about more than perfection; it's about making memories.
- Through cooking, teach your children that making mistakes is not failure; it is important to keep trying and, in time, you will succeed.
- Have a no rules policy at the table – talk about any topic to open the communication lines.

## THE HEART OF THE TABLE

Life is to be accomplished and lived in abundance. When we operate in this way, we find that we start to thrive not just survive. The heart of the table is the main artery, operating with all its cylinders and running smoothly, like a symphony.

Yes, there are always challenges in life, but they are only speed bumps. As a family, we work through them together and stay united through our struggles. Food brings families together and sharing food around the table becomes a ritual where you cannot wait to meet and share the day with each other.

We all play different kinds of music, but at the end of the day music is music and we are more the same than we are different. Create your own music, stay focused on what is the most important melody you want your family to sing and keep the harmony.

*What kind of music do you want to create across your table?*

..................................................................
..................................................................
..................................................................
..................................................................
..................................................................
..................................................................

# CHAPTER 15 – FAMILY AND HERITAGE

**Family and heritage are the core ingredients of who we are.**

Just this morning I was talking with my husband about how I used to sit with my Nonno Jack and listen to the stories he would tell me. My Nonno shared stories about truth, family and heritage, his life and his challenges and these experiences shaped him to become the pillar of strength in our family. He will never be forgotten. His grandchildren talk about him all the time and his presence is one that is noted along the generations of his great grandchildren even though they never met him in their lives, they know of him.

*Heritage is a reflection of our past. Family is the now.*

In the end, a person's story is what we remember most about them. Unfortunately, we will all die one day but most of us don't think about death so we don't appreciate what we have and how lucky we are to be able to live in the moment in such a blessed life. It is important to consider, while you are still alive, what story you want to tell with your life and how we want our family to remember us.

> To tell you where it all began
> 
> this is a story that is so grand.
> 
> It is of family and heritage
> 
> we all share in this message
> 
> we all play a part in this master plan.
> 
> Destiny is the shape of this hand
> 
> each sharing from this table
> 
> it will not end as just a fable!

In this chapter, I want to discuss how you can become a pillar of strength for your family. A pillar is the strongest supporter of your family – they stand out as a tower of strength, a rock, a bastion, backbone and champion.

The word 'pillar' comes from the Latin and means an integral part of the structure of a building – without a pillar the building will collapse.

For some of you, you will already be the pillar of your family. Without you, the family will be scattered, have no strength, no support and no foundations. In saying this, you need to be flexible and adaptable to change in the weather, depending on the conditions of the environment.

Think about a family who has built strength and endurance together because they went through something tough. Their future is secure. Being a pillar will create strength for your future generations and those of you who exist now. We are often stronger than we think. I would like to share one of my favourite sayings with you – Can you eat an elephant? Of course you can, if only you eat it in small, bite-size chunks.

## MAKING SPACE FOR WELLNESS

We have few pleasures in life and we constantly need to be reminded of them. Creating a space where nothing but pleasure can enter in our lives is one that requires diligence, persistence and perseverance. Once we practise this, we create habits that are long lasting and that benefit our wellbeing.

There is a place in all of us that we need to keep sacred; it is the place where we meet God. Keeping this place special and healthy is like being a gardener – it takes a lot of care to make sure the weeds don't destroy the produce, however, we can't get so caught up with the weeds that we forget about the flowers. Focus on the flowers and there will be no room for the weeds.

This place that you create within yourself is one where no one can come into, except for you and the divine God. When we become aware of our own wellness, we slowly start to nurture it and it radiates the treasure within us and spreads into our family and community.

## HOW TO BUILD MENTAL STRENGTH

- Firstly, you must believe in yourself. As a man thinks, so he is. You become what you believe about yourself.
- You must build the required mental energy and stamina to withstand hard times. Your emotional strength is something that will be collected along the way. As you get stronger, it is like a muscle, the more you use it, the stronger you will get.
- A mentally strong person strives to be kind, fair and pleases other people.
- Stay focused on the goals you want to achieve – not looking away from this is what makes you mentally strong.

## HOW TO BUILD EMOTIONAL STRENGTH

- Set reasonable goals and follow them. Make sure your goals are *SMART*:
    - *S* specific, significant
    - *M* measurable, meaningful, motivational
    - *A* attainable, achievable, acceptable
    - *R* realistic, relevant, reasonable, rewarding
    - *T* time-based, tangible and trackable.
- Be brave against negative thoughts. Negativity can come at you in different ways. It is important to be able to manage it; you might find it helpful to minimise contact with negative or toxic people. Choose to live every day as positively as you can – practising this will build emotional strength.
- Use positive self-talk to build your mental and emotional strength. Try this by telling yourself phrases such as:
    - I am working on becoming emotionally strong everyday
    - I will become better at managing my stress
    - I am closer to my goal of becoming emotionally and mentally strong every day.
- Learn to stay calm under pressure and know that you are in control of your emotions; they do not need to be the master of your life. Breathe, let things go; don't hold on to anything that you cannot control.
- Let go of the little things. Instead of stressing about a situation, develop a healthy habit of pausing to think what is actually bothering you, calm yourself down and decide on the healthiest, most productive way of dealing with it.
- Changing your thoughts will change your life. Your perspective is everything. Read more, volunteer your time, listen to a friend, and make sure you travel – it's good for the soul!
- Be in the moment during the happy times and enjoy your family and friends as much as possible.

Follow these steps and you will be on your way to becoming a person who is the pillar of your family. Life is a long marathon, but you are always a work in progress – you can do it!

Remember the story I told you in Chapter 1 about the man who was living on a diamond field? You are that treasure. All things are possible; it is your belief system that needs a check. We are always learning and shaping our diamond within to shine as bright as it can be.

I was struck by a commercial a few months from Ancestry.com. In the advertisement, there is a woman (who is supposed to be the viewer's long-lost relation) who stares at the camera and says, "come and find me". That is the essence of heritage. As soon as you start looking into your family's past, you actually start to find traces of you along the way.

**Write down the goals you want to achieve for yourself:**

..................................................................................

..................................................................................

..................................................................................

..................................................................................

..................................................................................

PART THREE: THE MUSIC OF THE TABLE

## LET'S RENDEZVOUS! THE FAMILY DYNAMICS

When I was a child and my parents were preparing the house for visitors, I was so excited I could not sleep the night before knowing that we would get to spend the next whole day with family. My mind would be bouncing around with how much fun we were going to have and the laughter that they would bring to the day; it was like adrenaline thumping in my veins.

I have aunties and uncles who have made my life so fabulous just by their sheer presence across the table. We could just be sharing a plate of simple food and, all of sudden, someone will either start an argument or crack up laughing – their personalities shine!

## MY FAMILY IS MADE UP OF CHARACTERS

My *zia* (auntie) Nina laughs so much that her whole body laughs and everything jiggles! She makes everyone's day. Her laughter is infectious and when she laughs, everyone at the table is laughing with her and you are mesmerised in the momentum of this wonderful rendezvous with her. Laughter and great company is what she brings to the table.

My friend Domenic Mandarano is someone I love to share the table with. He brings heritage, sayings that are centuries old and hilarious jokes to the table. It is virtually impossible to eat your meal without spitting it out in hysterics! When he speaks it's like generations speak through him.

He loves his garden and loves helping anyone in need and is always there for his friends and family. Domenic is my father's friend. They met in Sicily, where Domenic grew up in Isola Eolie, one of the islands in Sicily. He has family there still and often tells me the story of how he met his wife when he was an apprentice tiler and how he built a life around this experience. Rendezvousing at the table with Domenic is a pleasure as he brings generations of knowledge to the table.

My friend Paolo Mazzarella is also great to share the table with. I met him when I was about 4 years old and he is now 93 years old! He has perfect articulation and has taught me how to speak and be heard.

Paolo is also a writer and has written many articles and won many awards for his literature.

When we sit at the table together, Paolo has an infectious love for life that has only grown with age; it is truly inspiring. Rendezvousing with Paolo is priceless as he brings a wealth of language to the table.

*Have you ever had family members who make the table a place you don't want to leave?*

My auntie is what I would call the 'news broadcaster' of our family. She knows all of the local and international gossip and, if you spend a whole day with her you will know every birth, death and marriage of the family! I won't share her name here as it might offend her. She brings sheer joy and laughter to the table and she has a warmth that she shows by sharing every detail with you!

I could go on and tell you about so many members of my family and friends who I love to share a table with, but this is just an example to make you think about how much there is to gain by spending time with people at the table and to think about what you can also bring to the table.

Think about who you are and how you can stretch yourself across this magnificent table and share your own self and knowledge with the people you love. It's important to open yourself up and talk to those around you. Time is of the essence and we're not here for a long time, think about it. Seize the moment, live it, share it, breath it, rendezvous!

*Who is a person in your life that you can rendezvous with? Share this person's name with your children so that they will remember them too.*

..................................................................................

..................................................................................

..................................................................................

..................................................................................

*Now, set a date to catch up with them!*

THE HEART OF THE TABLE

# PART FOUR:
## The Wealth of the Table ♥

# CHAPTER 16 – A MEDITATION

The table has a heart. It has a voice from the past and one for the future. Your spirit and energy is centred there. Your presence is required at the table to start this heartbeat. Awaken! It's time, let's start! Seize this moment and unlock the treasure that is within you. Without a heartbeat, the heart cannot function. It's time to activate it. Tell your heart to beat again. Step into a new grace today.

*Join me in this meditation and feel its power:*

1. Place your hands on your heart. Sit and take deep breaths – this will help to re-centre your thoughts.
2. While you are being still, just think for a moment. Take hold of what is within you and capture this moment in time, it is so precious, let everything fade away.
3. If your thoughts are racing, try to quieten your mind and let them fade away.
4. Become the observer of your thoughts and allow them to pass you.
5. Think about your heart expanding and blossoming like a flower. Let your heart tell you the colour of your flower.
6. Think about your heart beating and working in full force. Let your heart talk to you and tell you its secrets, listen quietly.

Once you have practised this meditation, ask yourself the following questions:

1. What did you hear and think about when you listened to your heart?
2. Did you heart lead you to any goals you want to achieve?
3. Have you made an action plan for how to achieve your goals?

Take the time to meditate on your life, goals and achievements regularly and believe in yourself. You can achieve whatever you set out to do.

## A NEW JOURNEY

A new journey has begun. Every day is a new day to start again and you will only achieve your goals by *taking action*, not by just *thinking* about them. You are in control.

The heartbeat of the table is one that is critical to all of us; it's primary to the vital sign of your role here and your heart, paving a mission in it, and navigating the course without you being consciously aware. Without you, this course cannot be accomplished, there is no heartbeat.

Along our journey together, dear reader, we have experienced a new way of navigating through life and we have gathered the tools for how to communicate, collaborate and converse more successfully. Now, we are required to put it all into practise. Will you join me?

*Take hold of your steering wheel and take accountability for your actions and responsibility – it's time.* ♥

Words are important. When we put them into practise, words awaken our heart and tap into what has always been there from the start – creativity, generosity, freedom, laughing, talking, enjoying life, patience, kindness. These are the things we crave in life; these are the riches of our own personal treasures – this is what true wealth brings to the table.

Shape your future and join me as we walk on the awakened path that is already before us. Be ready for every moment and do not waste another day! When we look back on our lives, we will realise how short our time on this earth was. We cannot come back and rectify our mistakes but we can start now to create music for tomorrow.

Start your own movement and put your words into actions by inviting your friends and family to your table. Create memories through food – it's easy if everyone brings a plate and shares with one another.

# CHAPTER 17 – SHARING A MEAL

***The table is a place where we eat, meet and greet.***

I love when my friends drop by my place and gather around my table. They'll often bring a plate to share and this gives us an opportunity to bond at the table. These moments are as precious as diamonds. I also love it when my children come past and we share a meal. It gives me the opportunity to communicate with their souls through food.

I visited my Uncle Giovanni the other day and he wasn't feeling very well, so he was sitting in his lounge chair. However, the moment we started talking and sharing stories, his colour changed, he began to converse with us and we ended up visiting our cousins and he started to come to life again. This goes to show that people are not meant to be by themselves. It is so important to communicate with each other and constantly check in with our family and friends.

## EMBRACING FLEXIBILITY

It is important to remain flexible in our social interactions as, when we isolate ourselves, we get into a pattern of not wanting to stretch ourselves and make room for other people in our lives. I am guilty of this myself! Sometimes if friends drop by during meal times, and I've had a particularly hard day or week, I just want to sit down and have a meal. I don't want to do anything and I don't feel like cooking and sharing a plate of food with anyone – not because I don't want to see my friends, it's because I'm exhausted!

But then I realise that I am being selfish and need to be flexible to other people. The most important thing is to extend my own hospitality, share a meal with them, focus on their company and realise that they have dropped by specially to see Marco and me – that is truly special, isn't it? In the end, by having their company and sharing a meal with that friend, I forget about that week and we end up having great conversation and a fantastic time. This is what I call 'the shift' as I take the focus off me and include the 'we'.

## THE DOOR IS ALWAYS OPEN

In Sicilian families, a place at *la tavola* (the table) is an open invitation. Just as our doors are always open to friends, family and guests, we are also always ready to share a plate of food and are happy to have a conversation. The table is a glorious place to communicate; it's where we get to share what's going on in our lives and the more people we bring to the table, the better.

Each person brings something different to the table and we are all wonderful and unique in our own design. Sharing a meal together opens up and creates communication lines that extend it into the community. Not only that, but spending time with friends and family enhances our emotional and psychological health.

## THE COMMUNAL BODY

Each of our bodies is made up of trillions of cells. However, it seems that we have forgotten that we all share a communal body.

In my mother's hometown, when a local person was sick or in need, the townspeople would all gather together and cook a meal for the whole family. The town's generosity extended into the family's home, which created a strong sense of community and general wellbeing. That promise of support and strength is very important for society's happiness. What if we stopped acting this way towards others? It would be lost forever. Setting aside time to share a meal with loved ones creates seeds for tomorrow with a gift from today.

Let's continue this important tradition by becoming more flexible towards people. In this instance, it isn't the food that matters – it's about feeding the human spirit as we crave heart-to-heart contact and face-to-face communication. Our community and ability to share time with each other is psychologically, spiritually and emotionally the most vital part of being human. The connection of people begins at the table.

## THE SPIRIT OF CHRISTMAS

The year is 1970 and it's the Christmas summer holidays. I was 10 years old. The weather was hot and sticky and from my bedroom, I could smell the aromas of my Mother Sarina's cooking and the chatter in the kitchen from my Nonna Carmela. The delicious smell of cooking called me into the kitchen. At the table, I saw my parents, grandparents and my little brother Joe. The table was filled with all sorts of seafood: fish that dad had caught a few days before, lobster and crabs.

*The little girl who sat at that table with her family on Christmas day in 1970 is now a woman who wants to share the heart of the table with you.*

You couldn't even see the table as it was filled with so much food. This is a Christmas that I will never forget – it is still so vivid in my memory.

Why do I remember this Christmas so well? It is because we spent the whole evening talking, eating, laughing and connecting with each other. We joined together as one body, one cell, one memory and, decades later, it is still fresh and tangible in my mind. Aside from my brother and I, they have all passed away now, but the memories are alive.

By sharing meals, our experiences and memoires, we build a richer family and community for today and tomorrow. I urge you to imprint these words into your own mindset as this is what family and community are all about. I know that you care because together we have journeyed through this book, activating our mindsets and remembering what is truly valuable.

*Do you have a particular family memory that remains vivid in your mind? Note it down here:*

..................................................................
..................................................................
..................................................................
..................................................................
..................................................................

# CHAPTER 18 – THE HEART OF A WARRIOR

***Unlock your courage and let it beat like a lion's heart.***

A lion is an animal with great courage. Have you ever watched a documentary about a pride of lions – how they live and protect their own? Lionesses spend most of their day hunting and thinking about what they are going to eat next. The lion is the king of its domain; it has a strong spirit of leadership.

As leaders, lions differentiate themselves by their attitude. Leaders are not necessarily the tallest, largest, heaviest or smartest, yet they command respect. Leadership transforms the cowards into warriors because leadership determines everything. The lion is the king of the jungle because of its attitude – every other animal respects the lion because they have earned it with their fearless attitude.

## LIVING WITH A LION'S HEART

It's the heart I truly want to share with you in this book. I believe that deep inside all of us is the heart of a warrior. Imagine how different and amazing life could be if we decided to live our whole life with the same traits as a lion and with a lion's heart. There would be no boundaries. We would be fearless. Imagine what we could accomplish!

My nonno used to say, *"meglio un giorno da leone da cento da pegora"* (better a day as a lion than a thousand years as a sheep).

There you are, I can see you! Now that you're thinking like this, there is the real you on the other side of fear. Did you know that behind the fear is the person you really want to be?

*Step out of your comfort zone into the realm of the unknown. That is where life starts. Come join me.*

To create the heart of a warrior, we first must identify our purpose, cleanse our mindset, redirect our course and capture our higher purpose to empower us. Greatness takes time to develop, it is the treasure within us. Awaken your lion heart. The choice to be strong and courageous is one that you must make every day.

Throughout this book, I hope to have inspired you to open up the communication lines between you and your family and friends, and to start a new chapter.

## SETTING GOALS FOR THE FUTURE

The advice I have shared with you in this book comes from my own personal journey. I have mastered living with a lion's heart and aim to live my life like this every day. My story will connect with your story as we both try to live a strong and courageous life with clarity, honesty and generosity.

To live successfully with a lion's heart, it is important to set goals for the future so that you can be in control of life's challenges before they arrive.

This is all about building a great life for you and your family. My intention for you is to live and enjoy the diamonds of your days and create a life that, when you look back, you are satisfied that you have lived.

Ask yourself, "where do I see myself in 5, 10, 15 and 20 years?" Your answers to this question could result in creating a plan for you and your family. You are the only person who knows what you desire in life. Keep your hands on the steering wheel of your life. Take control of it and be authentic to your purpose. Doing this will take you back to the truth and realign you with your true self.

When you set out with a lion's heart and clear purpose, you will find that other people will be inspired by your actions and want to join in as well. Share your inspiration and help the people around you live their authentic lives. Give yourself openly to others and you will see it comes back to you in waves.

## THE CORE OF YOUR SOUL

The word *cuore* in Italian means heart. It's funny how the definition of core means, `the part of something that is central to its existence or character, primary, principal, main, fundamental, central, crucial, vital, essential'.

It's the main artery of the heart where the central existence and treasure resides – just as family and community are central to our happiness and wellbeing. When we live life with a healthy attitude, we are spreading positivity to our family and into the community.

I share my positivity and love by volunteering at the local school on Italian day. By sharing that day with the school's teachers and parents, we are united in our intention to create a day that is memorable for the students. I teach the school children about the staples of Italian cuisine – pizza and pasta – and they learn about my Italian heritage. The students spend the day buzzing around the school, dressed in their homemade Italian outfits and oozing with happiness. This joy flows through to their parents who are excited to see their children so happy and the teachers are also happy – it's a ripple effect that spreads through the whole school and into the community's homes, reaching across their kitchen tables.

This kind of volunteer experience makes me reflect on how we are all one body, sharing this amazing world. Imagine how strong a community will grow to be with the foundations of such a strong heart?

It's crucial that as we grow, we continue to share our time and energy with our community and touch other people's lives. The world is such a fantastic place, but it will always benefit from strong communities that pull together and help each other. Remember how my nonno would tell me that the seeds of the family will become strong trees?

The soul of the table is vital for all of our families to grow and be happy and healthy. The core of a happy heart starts in the home. That's why what we bring to the table is so important.

*A community spirit starts from our own lion heart.*

# CHAPTER 19 – COURAGE

*Sow courage and hope across the table.*

"Oh if I had the kind of faith that would move you!" said the mustard seed to the mountain. Is it possible for a small seed to move the mountain? How about if the seed has enough courage and hope and believes it can do it?

When it is just a small mustard seed, it was just a seed and couldn't see what it could become in the future. Everything that the seed needed to conquer the mountain was contained inside of itself, just as our own potential lies within us. We often search for strength outside of ourselves, unaware that we, alone, are enough. By allowing the process of life to unfold, we too will evolve – as will our purpose, vision and abilities. The mustard seed has the potential to become a large tree and it will be capable of a higher purpose.

C – communication
O – optimism
U – understanding
R – relationships
A – appreciation
G – gentleness
E – empathy ♥

By exercising courage and strong beliefs in your everyday life, you can achieve your goals and assist and mentor the lives of others.

Speaking words of courage into your life and into the lives of your children will help to grow the seeds of strength into your/their belief system. Your children will have the proper tools to overcome the challenges in their lives because you encouraged them to not be afraid.

In life, we often find it hard to see who we truly are and believe fully in our ability to accomplish goals. Just as the mustard seed could not see its future as a strong tree, we must also be patient and give ourselves time to grow before we can lead bold, meaningful lives.

If we listen to the voice of truth and have courage, we can live a life without fear. Putting this kind of positive self-talk into action continues to guide me to believe that I can achieve the goals I set for my family and myself.

Remember the proverb my nonno used to say to me, "better a day as a lion than a thousand years as a sheep". Living with a lion's heart requires courage, as the animal is so strong that with one wave, all things are possible.

Building courage on a day-to-day basis is like a workout, you cannot have a great body all at once, it takes time and patience and soon you see the results of the work you put in.

Have you ever heard the phrase, `When life gives you lemons, make lemonade'? I have my own version, 'When life gives Sicilian lemons, make limoncello!' We look at food like it's art – we see the colours, the shapes of the ingredients. We are courageous with our palate as we love to invent recipes and we aren't afraid to create unique dishes. It is important to be courageous in all that you do, not only in the hard times.

*When life gives Sicilian lemons, make limoncello!*

## HOPE

Hope is a word that people don't use much anymore, somehow it has become lost in the past. Have we forgotten its power? We can activate this word that is just there waiting to be used and as we use it in our daily lives it builds strength in us and our lives as we focus on our dreams – we should never give up hope.

Focus on what is important and let the rest of your worries fade away. It is important to always remain hopeful in everything you do. Share your hope at the table and see how the faces of your family will smile back at you.

My many years of hospitality have shown me countless faces and I have observed the energy that each person brings to their table. A person's attitude is their most important feature and I hope, for the future, that people (especially adults) remain hopeful and positive as other people (particularly children) observe our behaviour more than we know and they mirror what we say and do. Let's together instil hope, courage, strength and a voice of truth into our future leaders. This starts at our table.

*Be aware of your thoughts – what you think about all day is what you become.*

### FAITH

My faith builds strength in me and makes me feel as though I can move mountains. A good example of strength and faith is the story of David and Goliath. I'm sure you know the story, but if you need a re-cap, David was only a young shepherd boy with a sling in his hand, who had to battle against Goliath, who was a giant.

David had been building his muscles since he was a child and, in doing so, had acquired strength, precision and good timing by using his sling every day. On the day that David met Goliath, David would have felt sheer terror facing such a giant who was known for killing many soldiers. To make it worse, Goliath was taunting David with his words. But, David believed he could win this battle and, with just his sling and a rock, David struck Goliath dead.

Faith like David's will move mountains – he was just a shepherd boy who became the King of Israel. We too are kings and queens with warrior hearts, building our own courage, hope and sharing it across our table, spreading it into our families and communities.

**What are the 'mountains' in your life that you would like to change/move?**

..................................................................
..................................................................
..................................................................
..................................................................
..................................................................
..................................................................

**What do you believe is your purpose in life?**

..................................................................
..................................................................
..................................................................
..................................................................
..................................................................
..................................................................
..................................................................

# CHAPTER 20 – A JOURNEY THROUGH THE MARKET

*Leave a legacy of love across your table.*

Listen to the noises of the market
people talking, laughing.
Smell the fresh, crispy produce,
aromas of different ingredients and spices.
An energy of community,
and food, glorious food!
Are you ready?
Come on, let's go!

Come with me, let's take a journey to the market. There is so much I want to show you and tell you. Let's start by walking across the market to the fresh fruit market gardener, *il fruttivendolo,* who wakes up early in the morning to pick his fresh, crispy vegetables and chooses his fruit carefully to ensure that his customers enjoy the delicious flavours.

The sellers at the market work hard to keep their lands fertile so that the produce grows fresh and nutritious for their customers. They wake up early every morning to place their produce in the stall to sell. The thing that strikes me most is the vibrant colours of their produce – green, yellow, orange, red, brown, white, purple – so many wonderful colours to taste and feel the sensation of freshness entering my body, to nurture and keep me healthy. How dull life would be without these ingredients.

As we walk further, we see the local fisherman, *il pescatore*. His family has been fishing for generations and he has been up all night catching fish to sell at his market stall. Look at all those wonderful colours – silver, blue, shades of grey – shiny and fresh for us to pick up and look at while we talk to him. He recommends some fish for us to buy based on what will suit the recipe we want to cook for the day. You can see from his weathered skin how long he and his family have been fishing; he has a fire within his eyes that shows how proud he is of his catch and what he brings to the market.

As we keep walking through the market, the scenery evolves and we enjoy the fresh smells and aromas coming from the different kinds of produce. We next encounter the local shepherd and cheese maker, *formaggio artigianale* – his family has been making cheeses for generations. The smell of this market stall is wonderful as the cheese aromas float through the air, while our palates yearn for the delicious flavours on offer. We get to taste the fresh ricotta that bursts with flavours, slices of bocconcini and pecorino... there are so many choices of cheese, we don't know which one to taste and buy! As we consider our purchase, the market stall holder hands us a piece of fresh filone of pasta dura bread with cheese and the taste is divine. We savour this moment, as we have never tasted anything like this before.

**76** PART FOUR: THE WEALTH OF THE TABLE

The bread is from the local bread maker, whose stall is just next to his. We are so excited that we want to savour each moment and breathe in the market atmosphere. In this moment, we forget everything else and enjoy the wonderful experience we're having together.

The local baker, *panettiere locale del pane*, has too been up all night baking his bread. His family has been baking for generations and he is so proud of each loaf as it is his artistry for the community. The whole village goes to his shop and buys his bread – it is the freshest and crunchiest you have ever eaten, each bite makes you happy. His bakery is bursting with the smells of freshly baked bread, the whole village can smell it and everyone lines up to get some of his first batch of the day to eat with lunch.

We visit so many stalls and taste its produce. As we stop, we smell the local salami, *salumeria*, they are all lined and dangling outside the stall alongside the olives. We taste the local marinated olives and break a little of the fresh filone we just bought to savour this flavour.

You know, all of my worries are gone as we journey through the market together. There's nothing more enjoyable than sharing this experience with you and joining this community of people who are so passionate about their trades. If we need an ingredient for our recipes, we just ask the local shop owner and they will direct us to the supplier. Everyone is very hospitable and happy to assists us.

Hours have passed now and we have so many bags filled with delicious goods! To re-energise, we stop in at the local café for an espresso, a glass of water and a chat.

> *Spending time in the kitchen with you, laughing and smiling, is the best present you could ever give me.*

Sharing this day with you is priceless. As we look at all the food we have bought, the anticipation of cooking is so exhilarating and we decide that it is time to head back to our apartment and cook these meals together. As we say *arrivedeci* to the local people, we are filled with happiness from their hospitality and community spirit.

We arrive in our apartment, we decide to get started by cleaning and washing the vegetables before boiling them in water to blanch, as they don't need long to cook. We want to taste the freshness of these delicious vegetables.

While the vegetables are boiling, we place the fresh tuna in a frying pan and drizzle over some virgin olive oil that we bought at the market from the salumeria. We can smell the delicious aromas as we open the bottle! As we place the tuna pieces in the pan, they start to sizzle and we decide we are going to put a little garlic and diced parsley in the pan as well. The vegetables are ready, so we place them together in the frying pan with a little virgin olive oil, chilli and sea salt before tossing them around until they are ready.

While the tuna is cooking, we set our table with wine from the local mercato. This wine is made by a family from the next town who have been making wine for centuries. When we open the bottle, the aromas are bursting out to greet us. How divine.

*The wealth at this table is beyond our comprehension. As I take my first bite and sip my wine, I think to myself how life is so good with you at the table.*

Hey! The tuna is ready. We set the pan aside and slice the fresh bread. You can hear the crust cracking as the knife touches the bread. Next, we load up the table with all of the wonderful produce from the market, including fresh fruit for after our meal, and we add the tuna and vegetables last. We give thanks for the morning and the food we're lucky enough to enjoy.

Life could not get any better than this. Our friendship is made richer by sharing the love of food with each other.

Food with heart continues to beat through the generations, and this is made possible by the artisan makers we met at the market as they share their passion, heritage and culture with others through their produce.

As we dwell in this moment, ♥ I would like to pass a gift to you; a treasured heirloom. It has travelled from a continent for centuries, you cannot see it, but you feel it in spirit. It is what true wealth is made of – the treasure of family and friendship. I pass it to you from my Sicilian legacy. My parents brought this treasure with them, as they gathered together across their table, when they had no possessions. Yet, they had a richness that money cannot buy. Every person leaves this earth leaving a little of themselves behind, what do you want to leave behind?

# CHAPTER 21 – I LOVE YOU

*Say I love you across the table.*

I love you. When these words are spoken, they unlock freedom for the recipient as it allows them to feel, receive and give back. They are also powerful words for the person who is saying them as it opens the door to their heart, releasing the energy of love. Saying I love you can break chains of bondage as it removes the burden from the carrier. These words open up the channel of love in the word.

Learning to love myself has been a challenge in my life. For me, it is easy to love my children, parents, husband, brother and friends. Learning how to love myself, my own personal treasure, took time and patience. Ingrain the words I love you across the table, for all who sit with you, and share your table generously – this is how you leave a legacy for generations to come.

*With love comes freedom, mercy, grace, truth and joy.*

## LOVE IN LANGUAGE

Love is a word that has been watered down in many languages, especially in English. We use it so regularly in English it seems to have lost its meaning. In one breath, we can tell someone we love them and in the other we are saying we love chocolate, the beach or tennis!

But, love is more complex than that. Let's look at the word in other languages.

Ancient Greek philosophers identified four forms of love:

1. Familial love *(storge)*
2. Friendly love *(philia)*
3. Romantic love *(eros)*
4. Divine love *(agape)*.

The Latin language has several different verbs corresponding to the English word `love.' *Amo* is the basic verb meaning 'I love', with the infinitive *amare* (to love) as it still is in Italian today.

From the same Roman name comes *amicus* – friend, and *amicitia* – friendship in Italian is *amicizia*. The Latin uses the word *amare* where in English we would simply say 'to like'.

## SEWING LOVE INTO YOUR EVERYDAY LIFE

Incorporating love into your everyday life is up to you. 'I love you' are just words, but by acting upon them, you sew the seed of love in others and they will become truth from your effort. Love is a choice, an everyday engagement of joining together in union with the people around you.

Love is the universal connection between people and God; the desire to love and be loved in return is imbedded in our nature. Love is the key, we hold it in our hands and in our hearts. Become infectious, love everyone! Don't be held back by fear, you must learn why you fear such things and when you contemplate this you will learn more about yourself. When you come out of the other side of fear, you will see that it was there to teach you about yourself in order for you to grow.

*Taking action is like watering the seed to make love grow.*

If you feel as though you have forgotten who you truly are, it is love that will unlock the door and set you free. My affirmation to you is this: I am love and love is all around me.

You may not feel it. But I encourage you to keep walking in this affirmation and you will start to believe and when you look back you will see how far you have come. Watering the seed of an affirmation is crucial. Make time to affirm positive thoughts to yourself in the morning and in the evening. Believe in yourself and you will keep growing. May you see the love of who you really are and may God's light continue to flow brightly in you and through you. You don't need to go any further – you are enough.

## WHAT IS YOUR CALLING?

As we become more consciously aware of life, we realise that there is an urgency to discover our purpose before we leave this earth. We all have a special calling for our hearts and lives. A calling to be a better person, parent, friend, sister, brother, etc. As we better ourselves, we make the world a better place. You should always listen to your inner voice and listen to what it has to say, no matter how much it challenges you. Your life is a journey, my friend, and discovering your purpose is what life is all about.

*The calling is your spirit waking you up from sleep.*

Make sure you give yourself quiet, still moments so you can listen to your calling. Let the universe do its work in you, let it mould you like an artist moulds the clay. Trust the universe's intelligence to reveal itself and pave the way.

Everything will be okay, your course will unfold in the proper season and you will see in the end that all things happen for a reason. Just believe. The more you fight your purpose, the harder life will be. When you yield to it and let everything go, it becomes easier. Be the artist and the designer of your life. After all, that is what you came here to do – to expand, grow, create and allow your spirit to guide you through your journey.

Sit back and reflect on where you are in your life. Just think for a minute. Do you know that there is more to life than just working? What happens if you realise this too late? I don't think it's ever too late because whenever you actively change your life for the better, it is the right time for you. Your journey has taken you to this moment in time, to this destination to change your course. The time to act is now.

## REDISCOVER THE WONDER OF LOVE

Thank you for staying with me through this navigational guide that we have been on together. I would now like to speak more affirmations over you, to bless your life and purpose. It might be useful to read these affirmations more than once, especially when you may not be feeling as strong as usual.

May your life be filled with love and light, and your days filled with discovery and possibilities.

May you discover what your natural state of being is.

May everyday be an adventure and you will see the abundance of your surroundings.

May you rediscover your own love and be that love.

May you realise that you, yourself, are enough.

May you see the joy that you share around your table.

May you see that you are a miracle of life.

May you see the love that is around you everyday of your life.

May you see the reflection of the love that you have given and may it be given to you.

May joy and happiness surround you every day and it be spread through to your family and everyone that you touch.

May your life be filled with laughter and play.

May your mornings be adventurous before you create the day ahead.

May the peace and tranquillity of God protect all around you and your family all the days of your life.

May the peace of spirit remain steadfast in your life and continue to grow as you rediscover the love of life.

May you be empowered from the choices you make.

May your spirit be inspired as your journey in life continues.

May all of your dreams, hopes and desires unfold as you find your treasure.

May you see the treasure of your spouse, children, father, mother, sisters, brothers, cousins, nieces, nephews, aunties, uncles – your entire family and all of your friends.

May your table be surrounded with love and the wonderment of life.

And finally, dear reader, may you not be defined but be refined through your wonderful, unravelling experiences.

# CHAPTER 22 – WELCOME HOME

*Your family tree starts at the table.*

I have a question for you – what does home mean to you?

So many people in today's world think that home is made up of material possessions. But all of those things will fade away or go out of fashion and you will end up chasing rainbows and never get to that other side.

You are what makes your home special, as does the love inside that home. The treasure within us is waiting to make the house a home. Build a life that, when you look back on it, you are satisfied with your work and passion. Don't let anyone tell you that life is all about work, it isn't, we need balance. Home is a place where your roots can grow, be watered and fertilised and you can become the person you long to be.

## SICILY IS MY HOME

When I visit Sicily every year, I feel a sense of limitless strength and courage. It is the land and my heritage roots that give me strength to grow. When I am there, I feel one with the country, the people and all I want to do is become better to reach my full potential. It is like a power socket, when I attach the cord it's like BOOM! My heart and soul generate and thrive. It's not that I don't feel that way in Australia, but it is not as strong because Australia is my adopted home. It doesn't really matter whether you live in your home country or in a country that has adopted you. What matters most is what is important to you.

There is great strength in realising that you are your home. No matter where you are in the world, you can always count on you and if everything is great in you, then it extends all over the world – into your community and into other people's homes.

I have another question for you – What passions and dreams do you want to work on in the future?

*Home is not a place; it is a feeling. It is a place where we love, live and experience our lives.* ♥

This is something I often think about in my own life. I have this vision where all of my dreams are ghosts of the past and one day, when I cross over, they will come and reveal what could have been if I took the courage to achieve my dreams. In this space, I see my future self – the one who was held back for all of those years – and she says to me, "this is who you were meant to be and it's too late".

We all have many dreams we want to achieve in our lives, but it is up to you to make them happen. This is your calling. Achieving your goals takes time and you need the right tools to meet the challenge. Don't let the time pass you by without acting. Honour your calling and purpose in life, everyone has one, trust your heart.

We all have greatness in us; it opens the door to our purpose in life. When we focus on what we deeply love and are passionate about, we unlock our soul. When we tap into our soul's purpose, what we are on this earth to do, we start to live a life that is more full than we could have ever imagined.

What do you want your ghosts to reveal to you when you have completed your tasks on earth? I encourage you to write your story, sing that song, create the life you want to live, raise the bar in your business and never stop reaching for your dreams. You have nothing to lose; you only have the world to gain. Come on! Take a leap of faith and see how you will fly.

My purpose is to navigate you to the core of the heart of the table. My intention is to have a world where the family and community are at the heart of the table, for our children and our children's children.

## LIFE IS A DANCE

Look at life as if it is a dance. If we don't get up and learn the steps and practise, how will we learn this dance of life? We can sit in the pew and wait... but for what?

Take a partner and learn the dance of life. Throughout the learning process, we will need to ask for guidance and implement these new steps into our regime. Soon others will notice your steps and how well you dance. The more you dance, the better at life you will be and you will find new steps in your dance and shine like a star. The steps are within us. It is up to us to take the first step.

## MY VISION FOR THE FUTURE

There is a place in our hearts where our purpose resides and it is waiting for us to discover it. This purpose is our own personal treasure.

My vision is to create a movement that inspires the next generations to navigate and awaken their purpose. We all have different beliefs, desires and goals – it is up to us to bring them into fruition. To be in the best position to achieve our goals, we must connect with each other and seize the moment.

Life is not about gaining material possessions, it is about experiencing the diamonds of every day. Aim to create a world where:

- the table is an extension of our own into the community
- we can add an extra plate for a visitor
- we are happy to open our doors to other people.

## MY PURPOSE

My purpose is to inspire you to connect with your loved ones and unlock the treasure to the powerhouse of your table.

My intention is to help steer other people towards their own purpose. This will create a movement in the community that will become strong fertile soil for today and tomorrow.

### Why do I want to do this?

For the children who don't have their voice

For the adults who cannot find their own voice

For the devices that have taken over our communication lines

To remind you that every moment is as precious as the next

For the song that has never been sung

For the story that has never been told

For the dreams that never came into fruition

For the soul that only came to this earth for one moment

For the lonely people who sat and ate a meal alone at the table

For the people who are hungry

For the treasure that has not been found

For the meal that was never eaten

For the sick who craved for a meal that their mum used to make

For the men/women who sat in silence at the table

For the men/women who never spoke up at the table

For the voice of courage that never was taken up

For the hopes and dreams that were once at the table

For every opportunity that was missed

For you: to remind you that what we sow today is what we reap tomorrow

For all the nonnas/nonnos who desire for their grandchildren to live in a world where there is freedom to choose and be themselves

For all the immigrants who left their home countries to give their children the opportunity to build a new world – their selfless act became their legacy

For the times I remember when there was not enough food and my mother gave us what was on her plate and she would say "I am not hungry"

For the opportunities in my life that I never had the courage to take, enjoy and savour

For the times when I take an old recipe out and feel the connection of a passed loved one

For the treasure that lies within all of us

For the little girl who was not allowed to talk at the table

And for the woman who found her voice.

## THE FAMILY TREE

Come share with me
your legacy.
All from our
family tree.

In this plan,
we sow the tablecloth
of love across this land.

Spreading seeds of family and heritage,
they are the core ingredients of this recipe.
Your culture is the art
revealing the treasures of your heart.

The table is the place where
prayers are packed like nonna's lace
with grace.

Love is our light
to guide us
through the storms of our night.

The ingredients are sprinkled
with love to sow.
For this is all that will grow
together as we rest upon our family tree.

Sowing seeds in this land of Australia
we create a new memorabilia.
With a vision of a new table
that is strong and stable.
We open up our hearts so wide
with nothing to hide.

Sowing love into our community
a legacy of heritage and family
All from our tree
for all to see.

Master of Cucina Povera
Authentic Sicilian Cooking

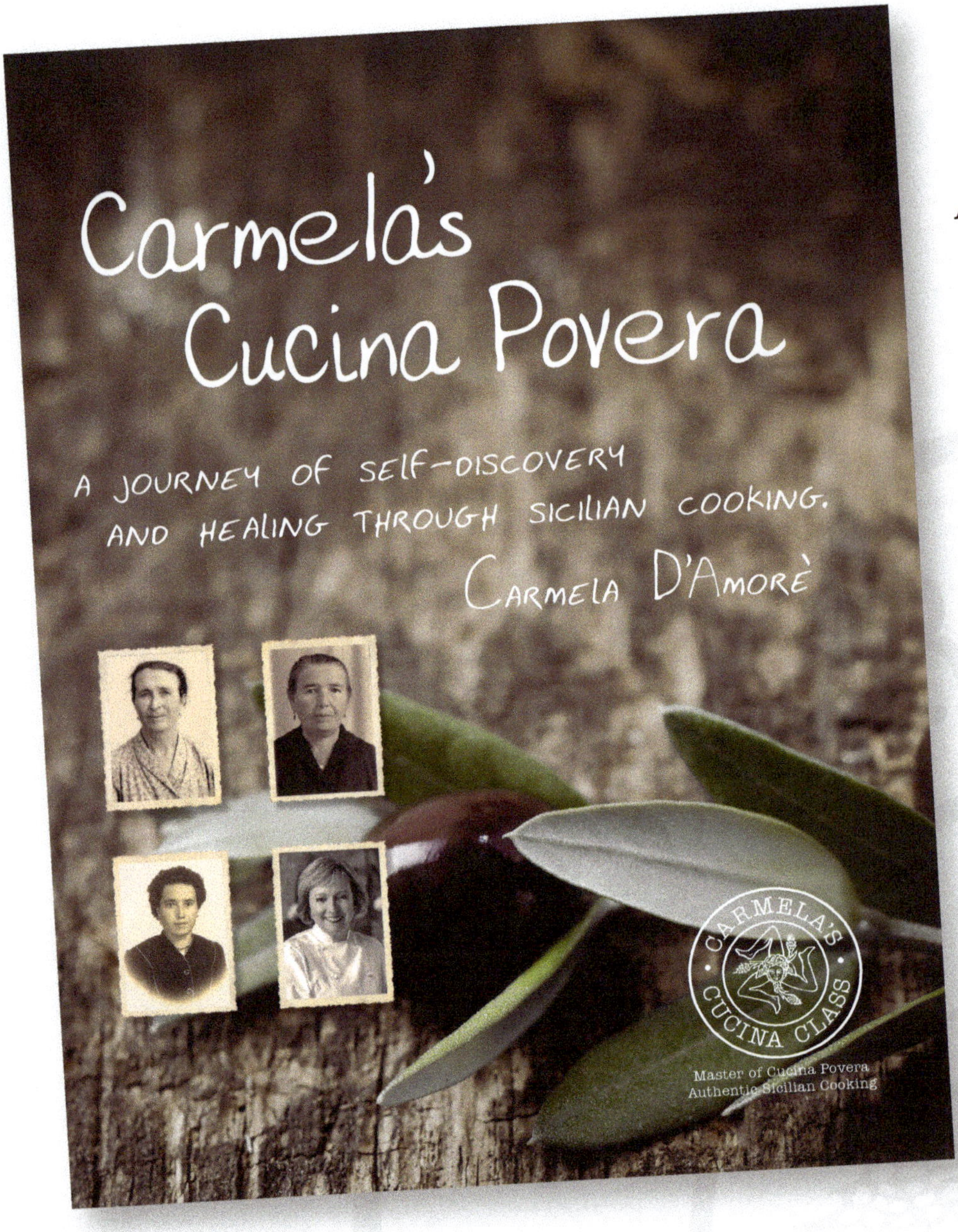

Read more from Carmela D'Amore by purchasing a copy of her first book, *Carmela's Cucina Povera: a journey of self-discovery and healing through Sicilian cooking.*

In this book, readers are taken on her journey of self-discovery and acceptance as she remembers, recreates and shares over 75 of her beloved family recipes from generations past.

Order your copy today at http://carmelascucinaclass.com.au/cookbook

www.ingramcontent.com/pod-product-compliance
Lightning Source LLC
Chambersburg PA
CBHW040752020526
44118CB00042B/2867